Erica Wilson's
CHILDREN'S WORLD

Erica Wilson's
CHILDREN'S
WORLD

Charles Scribner's Sons/New York

Library of Congress Cataloging in Publication Data

Wilson, Erica.
  Erica Wilson's children's world.

  1. Needlework.   I. Title.   II. Title: Children's
world.
TT751.W534   1983   746.4   83-14165
ISBN   0-684-18004-9

CONTENTS

If you were a cloud and sailed up there
You'd sail on water as blue as air,
And you'd see me here in the fields and say:
"Doesn't the sky look green today?"

A. A. Milne
from When We Were Very Young

"Stories in Stitches" might well be the title of this book, because it represents in needlework the delightful world of fantasy captured by some of our favorite children's books. Winnie the Pooh, Peter Rabbit, Babar, the Sunbonnet Girls, and, more recently, the Muppets™, are among the characters who people these pages.

These old friends, forever young, can be enjoyed by everyone from eight to eighty, and there's no doubt that our children and grandchildren will love them just as much as we and our grandparents did. To translate them into stitches means that we and our children can live with them as part of our familiar surroundings. How many of us remember the exact pattern on our quilt on the bed, the shape of the lamp, the wallpaper design in our own bedroom as we grew up?

On page 9, for instance, you will find a quilt that illustrates perfectly what this book is all about—storybook characters that everyone, regardless of age, finds irresistible. Here are Beatrix Potter's Peter Rabbit, Tom Kitten, Jemima Puddleduck, and their friends, appearing from the pages of a three-dimensional "book."

Precise instructions for each design are given throughout, but remember, nearly all of the ideas in this book are interchangeable. For example, if you prefer counted cross-stitch instead of painting for the quilt on the next page, refer to the method on page 134. If you would rather work the design in appliquéd fabric, follow the instructions for the appliqué bib on page 38. In this way you can use the patterns throughout the book interchangeably and make your own creations in your favorite technique.

BEATRIX POTTER

It all began with a letter to a little boy who was sick in bed. Beatrix Potter, who wrote the letter, made up a little story about rabbits, illustrating it with sketches, to cheer him up. How could she possibly imagine that nearly one hundred years later her stories would be translated into fifteen languages and enjoyed by millions all over the world?

Though it seems disarmingly simple, Beatrix Potter's quick sketches in her letter were the result of a lifetime of living with animals, studying a drawing from the skeleton up. As Sir John Millais, to whom Beatrix was apprenticed, said, "Anyone can draw, but you have the gift of observation."

About ten years after she wrote the letter to the little boy, and after having been turned down by six publishers, Beatrix had *The Tale of Peter Rabbit* privately printed, at the insistence of her friends. When the publisher Frederick Warne wrote to her about his publishing it, she modestly wrote, "I am aware that these little books don't last long, even if they are a success."

Perhaps they were a success because, in her own words, they were created especially for individual children, not "made to order," or, in present-day terms, made for "mass production." At age fifty, Beatrix wrote: "I have first made stories to please myself because I never grew up. . . . My usual way of writing is to scribble and cut out, and write it again and again. The shorter and plainer the better, and read the Bible if I feel my style wants chastening."

Translating her classic stories into needlework can be a kind of apprenticeship. As you stitch you learn to appreciate the work of an artist who is ageless, because of her great simplicity and ability to invest the animals with human traits without their losing their individual animal characteristics.

"ONCE UPON A TIME" QUILT

(Color Plate 1)

You can easily (and quickly!) make this charming storybook quilt by painting or stenciling each animal on a separate piece of fabric. You then cut out each one, pad it to make a little flat pillow, and then stitch it in place on the quilt. Alternatively, you can use Velcro fasteners so the position of each animal can be changed or removed for washing. The new paints are completely permanent, and you can throw the quilt into the washing machine without fear of the color running. The paints set without hardening the fabric, so you can add the finishing touches of embroidery and quilting afterward. If you baste a sheet of quilt batting behind the painted design, then outline each shape with stem stitch or backstitch in cotton floss, your painted design will have the attractive effect of appliqué and no one will quite know how you did it. Finished quilt measures 37 x 48".

MATERIALS

Size 5 stencil paint brush
Acrylic paint *(see* Suppliers)
100% cotton or 50% polycotton prequilted broadcloth: 1½ yards for animals, 1½ yards for quilt
12" Fanny Frame or stretcher bars
Clear or frosted heavyweight acetate—.005 weight is average—or self-adhesive stencil material *(see* Suppliers)
Rubber cutting mat *(see* Suppliers)
X-acto cutting blade, hobby knife, or sharp-pointed scissors
Felt-tipped permanent marker
Cotton floss
Quilt batting
Tailor's chalk pencil

ORDER OF WORKING

Begin by stenciling (see steps below) or appliquéing the fabric. Next, add touches of embroidery (see below). Finally, quilt and then finish the quilt.

1 square = 1 inch

Stenciling

- Prepare the stencil by laying heavyweight acetate or self-adhesive stencil material over the designs on the following pages. Trace the designs with a fine-tip permanent market.
- Tape the tracing to a rubber cutting mat or a piece of glass. With an X-acto blade, hobby knife, or sharp scissors, carefully cut out the shaded areas.
- Take care not to cut through narrow intersections between areas, so the result is a complete stencil with separate open areas. (Accidental cuts or breaks can be repaired with Scotch tape.)
- Stretch the fabric wrong side up in a Fanny Frame or on stretcher strips (page 129).
- Lay the stretched fabric wrong side down on a layer of paper towels, newspaper, or blotting paper so that it lies flat.
- Place the stencil in position on top and tape firmly to prevent slipping.
- Choose your first color for painting (the lightest is best), and block off with masking tape any adjoining open sections. Change tape with each color.
- With the stencil brush, paint each color, using the "stippling" technique. Do not make smooth strokes with the brush; instead, press it straight down on the cloth with small sharp movements to ensure penetration. Make sure the paint goes up to the edge of the stencil and not beyond.

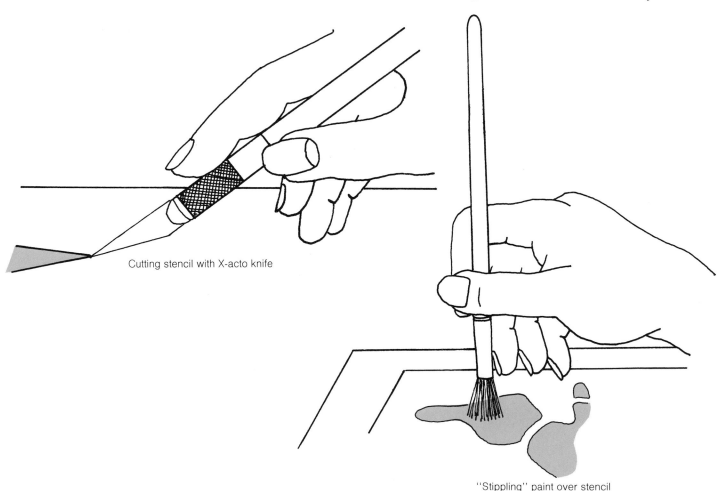

Cutting stencil with X-acto knife

"Stippling" paint over stencil

Embroidery

- Trace sections for embroidery on Trace Erase™ fabric and baste on top of fabric.
- Work embroidery details using 2 strands of cotton floss.
- Work details, such as padded satin-stitch eyes, buttons, French knots to represent spotted fabric, frills on aprons in French knots on stalks, turkey work on tails, etc. Do not work any outlines.

Quilting

- Baste batting and muslin on reverse side of design (some batting makes muslin unnecessary; *see* Suppliers). Outline animals in stem stitch, backstitch, or a combination of the two, working through the three layers of fabric.
- Stitch backing, right sides facing, all around, leaving a small opening for turning inside out. Stitch opening closed.
- Attach Velcro to animal and quilt.

12

13

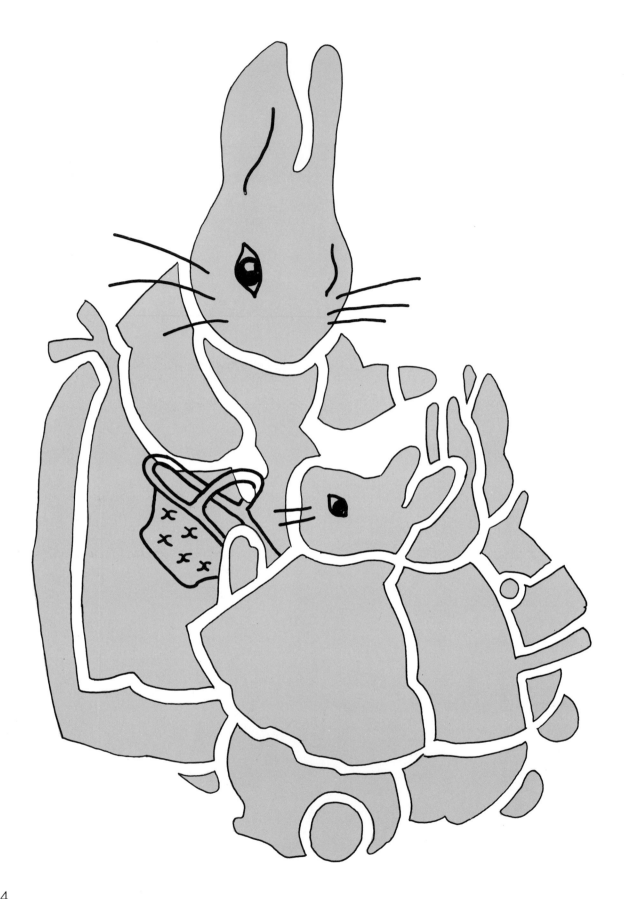

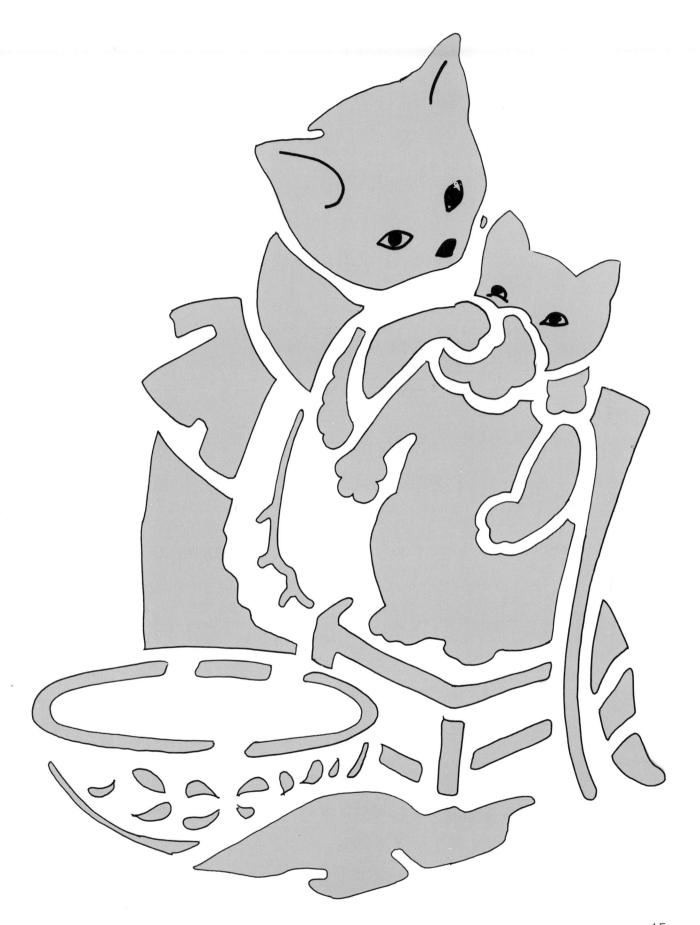

1 square = 1 inch

CATS WASHING

(Color Plate 7)

Acrylic paints are the quick and easy way of putting a design on fabric for a shower curtain, wall hanging, or quilted bedspread. After the paints are dry, add embroidery details and quilting, and the finished piece will have the effect of appliqué.

MATERIALS

Cotton or polyester fabric
Batting
Quilting thread
Cotton floss
Two 22″ and two 24″ stretcher strips
Acrylic paints (*see* Suppliers)

ORDER OF WORKING

- Enlarge pattern to desired size (panel shown is 22 x 24″).
- Stretch fabric on artists' stretcher strips.
- Trace enlarged pattern with hard "H" pencil on fabric (see page 131).
- Use acrylic paints to paint each area, following Color Plate 7 or use your own color scheme.
- Medium shades are shown by toned areas on chart. Shading and highlights can be added with dry brush strokes on top afterward.
- When paints are dry add embroidery details, such as padded satin-stitch eyes and nose, French knots on sponge, straight stitches for fur, etc.
- Back first with batting, then with muslin, and quilt around main outlines with running stitch.

16

Plate 1. "ONCE UPON A TIME" storybook quilt (page 9).

Plates 1–11 are projects based on Beatrix Potter characters, reproduced by permission of Frederick Warne, Publisher.

2.

3.

Plate 2. "HICKORY DICKORY DOCK" cross-stitch clock (page 26).

Plate 3. "THE LITTLE OLD LADY WHO LIVED IN A SHOE" pillow (page 30).

Plate 4. "STITCHING MOUSE" sewing basket (page 28).

Plate 5. Detail of sewing basket (Plate 4) pin-cushion lid.

Plate 6. "GUINEA PIG GARDENERS" frilled crewel pillow (page 32).

Plate 7. "CATS WASHING" shower curtain design (page 16).

Plate 8. "MY KNITTING BAG" and "HUNCA MUNCA AND BABIES" pillow (pages 35–36).

5.

4.

6.

7.

8.

Plate 9. "RUN RABBIT RUN" sweater (page 17).

Plate 10. Detail of sweater (Plate 9).

Plate 11. Beatrix Potter plastic canvas blocks and mini-sweaters for furry animals (pages 18–19).

RUN RABBIT RUN

Peter Rabbit in his little blue sweater can be worked in so many different ways, using the charts here for cross-stitch, needlepoint, and even a latch-hook rug. Repeated around the bottom of a sweater, Peter can be worked in duplicate stitch, either on a store-bought sweater or one you have knitted yourself (see below).

While you're knitting, you could make a little minisweater for a favorite furry animal. The knitting stretches so it could be made for any rabbit approximately 6 to 10 inches tall (see page 18).

When it comes to gifts for the baby, blocks made of plastic canvas are quick, easy, and fun to make. The charts shown here fit on squares 5¼ x 5¼", but you could adapt any of the other cross-stitch animals in this book to make blocks of different sizes. For a finishing touch, before sewing the final side in place stuff the block with lightweight batting, and put a bell inside (see page 19).

PETER RABBIT SWEATER

(Color Plates 9 and 10)

The Peter Rabbit sweater opposite was stitched in four strands of cotton floss on a store-bought cotton-knit sweater. Designs in duplicate stitch look as if they were knitted in but are actually stitched on top afterward.

MATERIALS

Cotton floss
Blunt tapestry needle
Floss or yarn of comparable weight to knitted garment

ORDER OF WORKING

- Follow colors in Plate 10 and count stitches from the graph.
- Bring needle up at the base of the stitch to be covered.
- Pass needle from right to left under two loops of the same stitch one row above.
- Reinsert needle into the base of the original stitch.
- Pull each stitch gently to maintain the tension of the original knitting, completely covering stitches with the new color.

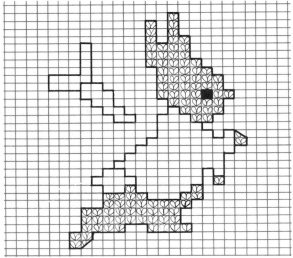

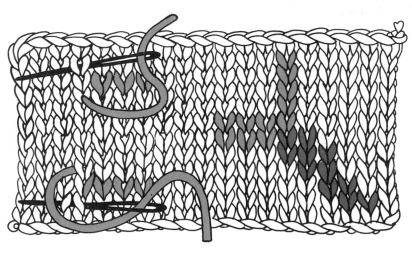

MINI TURTLENECK

(Color Plate 11)

The little turtleneck sweater shown opposite and in Color Plate 11 measures approximately 8″ around and 2½″ from shoulder to waist, so it will fit a 6 to 7 inch stuffed animal. It is knitted in one flat piece, then joined at the side seams and underarms to make it simple and quick to knit.

MATERIALS

1 oz. baby yarn

#3 knitting needles, 1 pair straight and 1 pair double pointed (or size to obtain correct gauge)

Gauge: 13 sts = 2″ (stockinette stitch)

ORDER OF WORKING

- With straight needles, cast on 26 stitches.
- Rows 1–4: Work even in k1, p1 ribbing.
- Rows 5–12: Work even in stockinette stitch (k1 row, p1 row).
- Row 13: Cast on 6 stitches for beginning of row and k32.
- Row 14: Cast on 6 stitches for beginning of row, then k2, p34, k2.
- Row 15: k38.
- Row 16: k2, p34, k2.
- Rows 17–30: Repeat rows 15 and 16.
- Row 31: k10, bind off 18, k10.
- Row 32: k2, p8, cast on 18, p8, k2.
- Rows 33–48: Repeat rows 15 and 16.
- Row 49: Bind off 6 stitches, k across.
- Row 50: Bind off 6 stitches, p across.
- Rows 51–58: Work even in stockinette stitch.
- Rows 59–62: Work even in k1, p1 ribbing. Bind off.
- Sew sleeve and side seams.
- Turtleneck: Pick up 36 stitches from front and back neckline and divide evenly over double-pointed needles. Work 12 rounds of k1, p1 ribbing. Bind off.
- Add pom poms on twisted ties (see page 152).

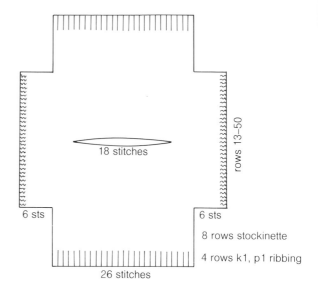

18 stitches

rows 13–50

6 sts · 6 sts

8 rows stockinette

4 rows k1, p1 ribbing

26 stitches

PLASTIC CANVAS ALPHABET BLOCKS ————

(Color Plate 11)

MATERIALS

To make blocks with sides 5¼" square:
2 sheets plastic canvas, 7 holes to the inch
  (10½ x 13½") for each block
Crewel wool
18 tapestry needle
Batting
Bell (optional)

ORDER OF WORKING

- Cut 6 squares of plastic canvas, measuring
  5¼ x 5¼".

- Work entire block in half-cross stitch
  following the graphs.
- If you use a white background, work that
  first, still counting from the graphs. In this
  way, small pieces of colored wool will not
  become enmeshed with the white, and the
  background will stay clean. Establish the
  center of each block and baste the outlines
  of the alphabet letters, if you prefer, before
  working the background.
- Join the 6 squares to form a block with
  lacing or joining stitch in a contrasting color.
- Before joining the last side, stuff with batting and add a bell.

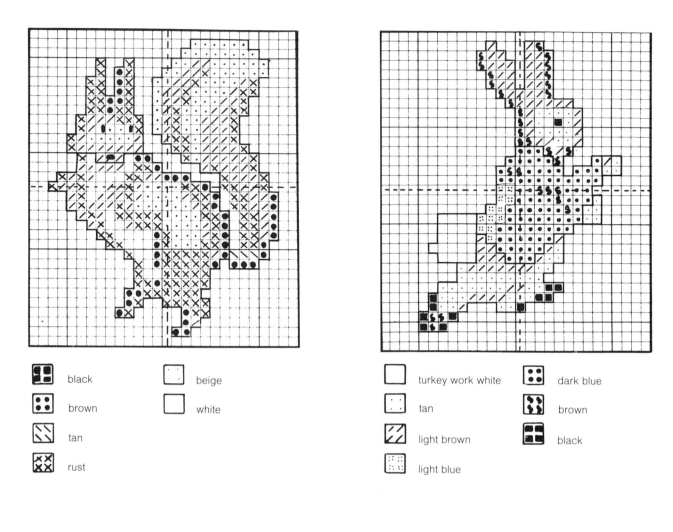

Symbol	Color
▣ (black squares)	black
⊟ (dots)	brown
⧄	tan
⊠	rust
⊡ (single dot)	beige
☐ (blank)	white

Symbol	Color
☐ (blank)	turkey work white
⊡ (dots)	tan
⧄	light brown
⊡ (small dots)	light blue
⊟ (four dots)	dark blue
⧅	brown
▣	black

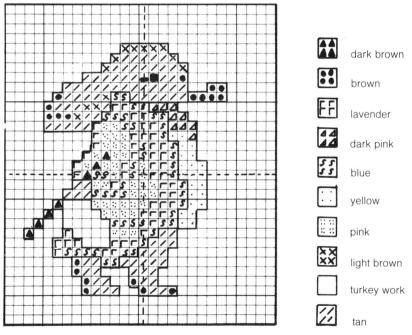

Symbol	Color
▲▲	dark brown
⊟	brown
FF	lavender
⧄⧄	dark pink
ʃʃ	blue
⊡	yellow
⊡	pink
⊠	light brown
☐	turkey work
⧄	tan

20

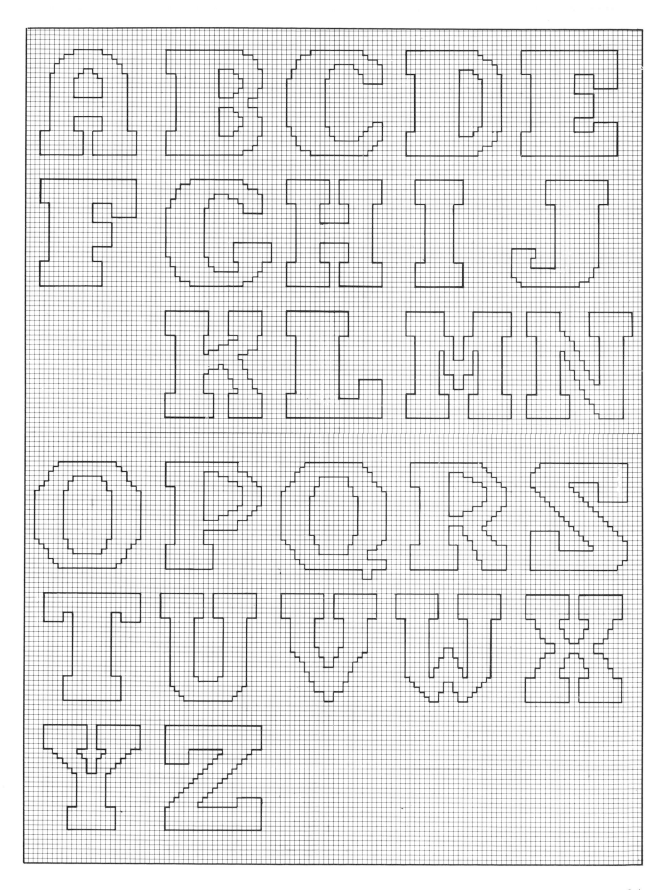

21

LOVE IS A SHARED UMBRELLA

Large scale brings out the texture of crewel stitches in this picture, which measures 28 x 33″. Worked in cross-stitch, it could be used for the bib of an apron, as shown, as a frilled pillow like the gardening guinea pigs on page 32, or even used on the front of a T-shirt, as with the Wind in the Willows sweat shirt on page 82.

MATERIALS FOR CREWEL PICTURE

Two 32″ and two 38″ stretcher bars
1 yard heavy natural linen
Crewel wools
18 chenille needle
Rug needle

ORDER OF WORKING FOR CREWEL PICTURE

- Enlarge and transfer the design on page 25 (see page 131 for transferring designs).
- Mount the design on stretcher bars.
- Using 3 threads, unless otherwise noted, work the stitches, following the diagram on page 25. On that diagram, letters refer to stitches, numbers to colors.

MATERIALS FOR CROSS-STITCH

Aida cloth (any size; photo shows 8 threads to the inch; finished design measures 6½ x 9″)
Cotton floss
20 Tapestry needle

ORDER OF WORKING FOR CROSS-STITCH

- Count out the stitches using a blunt tapestry needle and 4 threads of floss on # 10 Aida cloth. When cross-stitch is complete, backstitch all edges in dark green, dark brown, or dark blue floss to coordinate with each shape, using 1 or 2 threads. Work lettering in stem stitch using 3 threads.

- Colors are: umbrella top—light green; underneath—dark green; shaft—gold; rabbits—light, medium, and dark brown; eyes—black and white; Mrs. Rabbit's coat—red and pink; apron—light and medium blue and white; flowers—red, orange, and blue; Peter—light, medium, and dark blue jacket; vest and buttons—gold; basket—yellow; carrots—orange; grass—light and dark green; lettering—blue.

MOUNTING See page 137.

YARN COLOR KEY

Yarn No.	Color Name
1	Med. orange
2	Bright orange
3	Peach
4	Dk. peach
5	Lt. yellow
6	Bright yellow
7	Med. yellow
8	Lt. blue
9	Med. blue
10	Blue
11	Bright blue
12	Navy blue
13	Celery green
14	Lt. olive green
15	Mint green
16	Kelly green
17	Olive green
18	Dk. green
19	Lt. beige
20	Dk. beige
21	Flesh
22	Lt. brown
23	Med. brown
24	Dk. brown
25	Dull orange
26	Brick red
27	Black
28	White

STITCH KEY

Stitch Letter	Stitch Name
A	Long & short
B	Stem stitch
C	Backstitch
D	Satin stitch
E	Straight stitch
F	Laidwork
G	Raised chain stitch
H	Open chain stitch
J	French knots
K	Turkey work
L	Couching

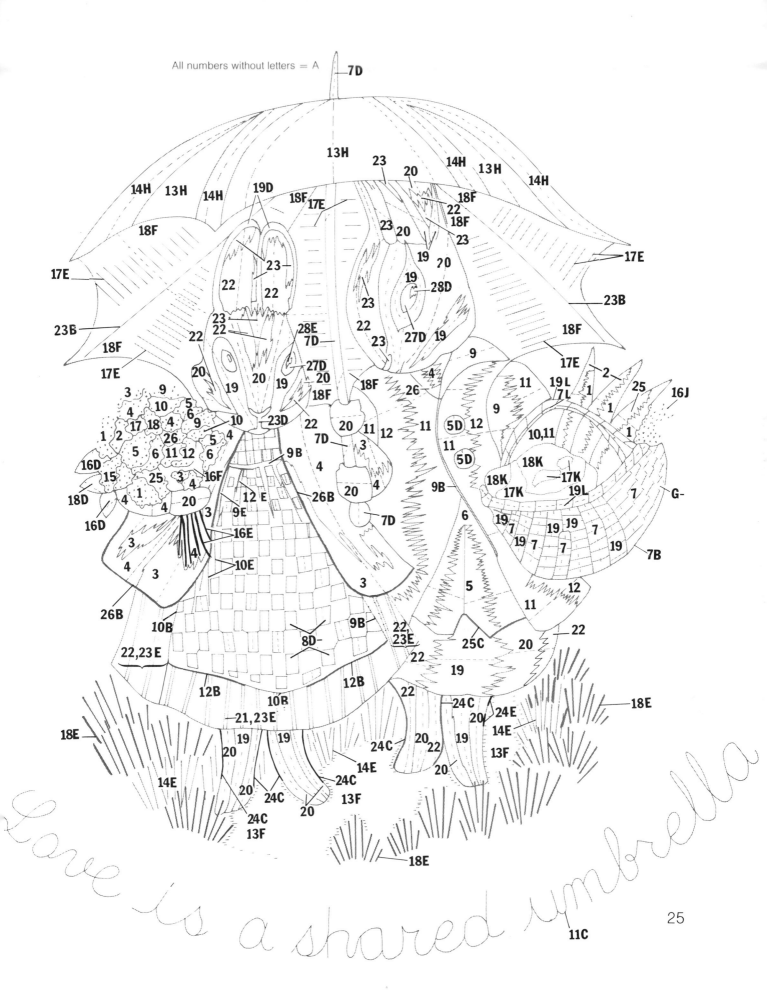

All numbers without letters = A

25

HICKORY DICKORY DOCK

(Color Plate 2)

This clock with Beatrix Potter's playful animals in cross-stitch may be framed as in Color Plate 2 or mounted in a simple square picture frame with a battery-driven clock mechanism behind. As you can easily imagine, the design would be equally attractive used as a picture, photo, or mirror frame, as the padded cover of a baby's first book, or as a birth sampler with the child's name and date and place of birth in the center.

MATERIALS

14 x 16″ cream # 14 Aida cloth
Cotton floss
20 tapestry needle
Battery-driven clock movement (*see* Suppliers)
Frame with approximately 9 x 12″ inner measurement

ORDER OF WORKING

- Establish the center of the fabric by basting with contrasting thread in both directions.
- First count the pattern from the graph, then outline with backstitch, working over 1 or 2 threads of the linen, as in the photo, with a single strand of black floss in the needle.
- Separate the 6-strand floss, and work in cross-stitch with 3 strands, following the diagrams. Fill in each area, referring to the graph opposite and Color Plate 2.

MOUNTING

- Temporarily wrap the plywood or board with finished embroidery to establish the center of the dial. Mark with a needle or pinpoint right through to the board. Remove needlework and make a hole in the board large enough to allow clock mechanism to come through.
- Cover board with thin batting. Secure with masking tape.
- Cover with finished needlework and secure in the same way.
- Pierce small hole in fabric where clock mechanism should penetrate. Fix hands in position.
- Frame in shadow-box frame to allow clock to hang clear of mechanism.
- For alternate use as a birth sampler, follow the alphabet graph on page 35.

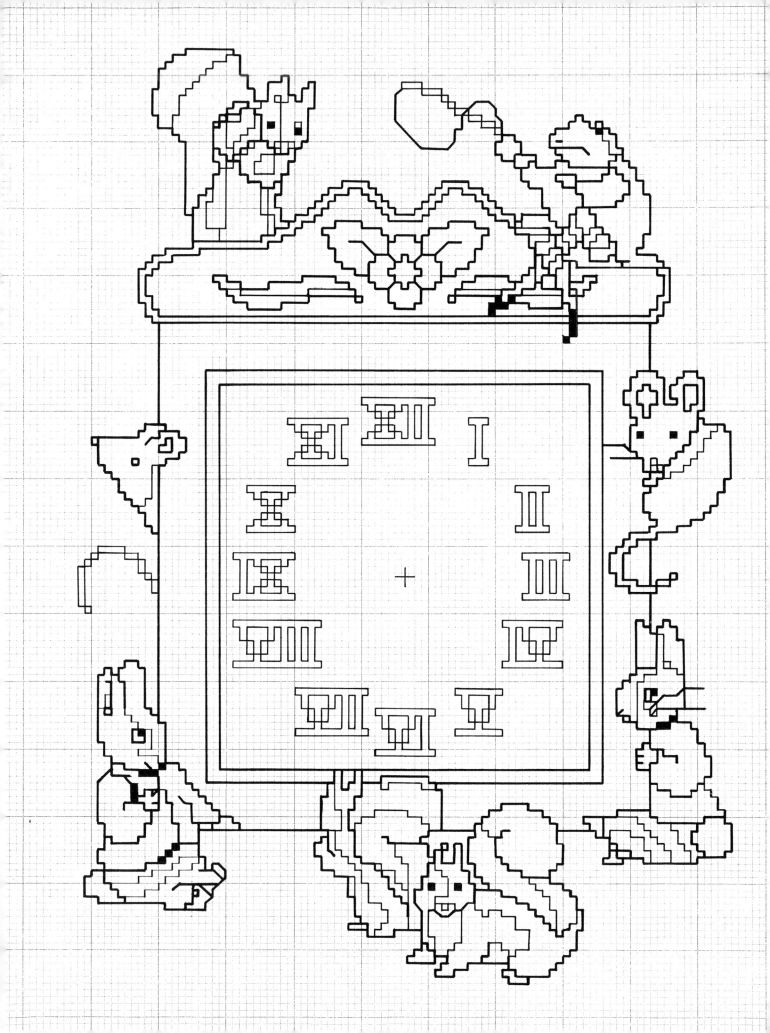

STITCHING MOUSE

(Color Plates 4 and 5)

"The Tailor of Gloucester" is one of Beatrix Potter's most delightful tales. Whilst the tailor lay sick in bed, the mice stayed up and finished the embroidered coat for the Mayor of Gloucester just in time for Christmas day. The design seems perfect for the padded pincushion lid of a sewing basket. With a little imagination we might find the mice finishing *our* needlework if we leave it nearby!

MATERIALS

12 x 12" natural color linen or cotton fabric
Crewel wools/cotton floss
#8 crewel needle
½ yard fabric for frill and lining of basket
Painted or plain basket with 6½" diameter

ORDER OF WORKING

- Trace the life-size design and transfer to the fabric (page 131).
- Work the design in one thread of crewel wool or 3 threads of cotton floss or a com-

bination of the two. Mouse: long and short stitch. Start at the top of the head, shading from dark to lighter shades. Work ears, starting at top of each, directing stitches toward base of ear. Eyes: Padded satin stitch. Whiskers and needle: stem stitch. Tail: slanting satin stitch. Mouse at left, flowers to right: long and short stitch. Flowered chintz: stem stitch and lazy daisy.

MOUNTING

- Cut a circle the diameter of the basket in cardboard.
- Pad with batting.
- Run gathering thread around finished embroidery.
- Draw up gathering thread around cardboard circle with batting.
- Attach contrasting frill and trim away excess fabric.
- Line, hemming the lining around circumference just inside the edge underneath pincushion top.

THE LITTLE OLD LADY WHO LIVED IN A SHOE
(Color Plate 3)

"You know the old lady who lived in a shoe
Who had so many children she didn't know
   what to do?
I think if she lived in a little shoe house
That little old lady was surely a mouse!"
               —BEATRIX POTTER

You can work this crewel pillow on linen and coordinate it with the coloring of your room by framing it first with a narrow band of fabric, then add a pleated frill as a final touch (page 137). Alternately, work it in cross-stitch.

MATERIALS FOR CREWEL

1 yard linen or cotton fabric

Crewel wool (1 strand throughout except 2 strands for French knots and knotted pearl stitch)
18 chenille needle/ # 18 tapestry needle
80″ strip of 5″ wide fabric for ruffle
Two 19 x 2½″ strips
Two 21 x 2½″ strips
One 19 x 21″ strip for backing
One 20 x 22″ pillow stuffer
Contrasting fabric for mounting (*see* Suppliers)

ORDER OF WORKING

- Enlarge and transfer design to fabric (page 128).
- Mount fabric in Fanny Frame (page 130).

30

- Work stitches following chart. Numbers show number of threads to use. For colors, see Plate 3 or use your own color scheme.

STITCHES

Shoe: vertical long and short stitches. Lace on shoe: French knots, buttonhole. Mice: vertical long and short. Eyes and nose: padded satin stitch. Whiskers: stem stitch. Tails: knotted pearl stitch. Mrs. Mouse's bonnet: vertical long and short. Lace bonnet: French knots on stalks.

- Work all vertical long and short stitches first.
- Outline the upper section of each area first with split stitch.
- Work over this outline in long and short stitches.
- Complete each area before outlining and working the next.
- Add all details, such as features, whiskers, and tails, lace in French knots and French knots on stalks last, overlaying them on top of previous stitching if necessary.

THE GUINEA PIG GARDENERS

(Color Plate 6)

Make the "gardeners" into a frilled crewel pillow, a picture, or the top of a mirror. Surround it with your favorite verse to make a perfect gift for a gardening friend.

MATERIALS

13 x 16" linen or cotton fabric (finished size 9 x 12")
Crewel wools
#20 chenille needle (or #8 crewel)
½ yard fabric for ruffle and backing (finish width of ruffle: 2")

2 yards eyelet ruffle (finished width: 1")

ORDER OF WORKING

- Trace and transfer the full-size design opposite to fabric (page 131).
- Work the stitches, using 1 thread of crewel wool, following Color Plate 6.
- Using Trace Erase™ fabric, transfer your verse to your design (page 132).
- Block and mount (page 137).

We love our little garden ~ and tend it with such care ~

You'll never find a faded leaf ~ or blighted blossom there.

33

MY KNITTING BAG

(Color Plate 8)

The knitting mouse could be worked in cross-stitch as shown in the photo, or use the graph to stitch her in needlepoint. An ideal use for either is the front pocket on a strong duck tote bag to hold—what else—knitting, of course!

MATERIALS

8-to-the-inch white Aida cloth 14 x 16"
1¾ yards green heavyweight fabric
½ yard finely checked gingham
7 yards ⅜" embroidered ribbon to match
¼ yard heavyweight interfacing
Cardboard 5 x 15"
#20 tapestry needle
Cotton floss

ORDER OF WORKING

- Count cross-stitch from graph, separating the 6-strand floss to use 4 threads.
- Outline with backstitch using single-thread black floss.
- Center and mark with basting the position of your lettering and count and stitch it from the alphabet chart below.

MOUNTING

See page 138.

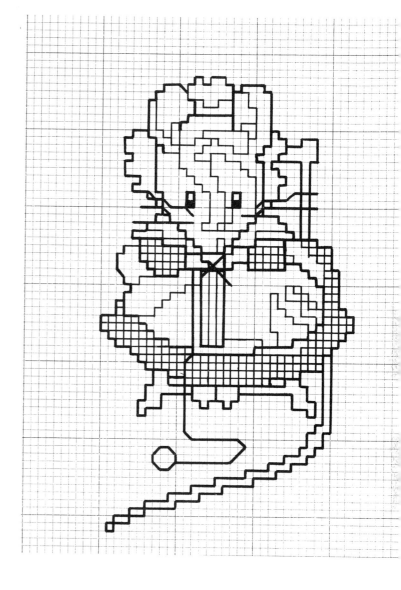

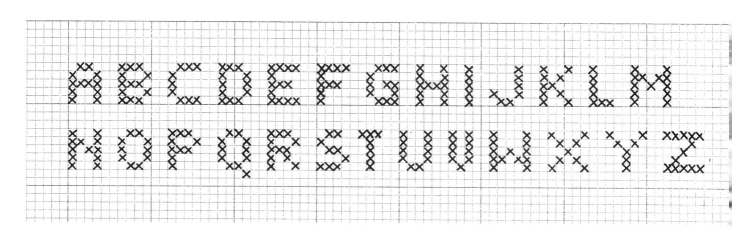

HUNCA MUNCA WITH BABIES

Color Plate 8)

Hunca Munca stole into the dolls' house and borrowed their cradle for her own babies. Here she is rocking them to sleep under a snug blanket. Shown here as a pillow, it would also make a charming birth sampler, changing the blanket from pink to blue as necessary (and, of course, the number of babies in the crib!).

MATERIALS

8-to-the-inch Aida cloth 18 x 18"
 (finished size: 14 x 14")
#20 tapestry needle

Cotton floss
1 yard calico for backing and ruffle
2½ yards eyelet for ruffle

ORDER OF WORKING

- Using the graph below, count out the design in cross-stitch, starting from the center point (marked with an X on the chart).
- Separate the 6-strand floss and use 4 threads in the needle.
- Outline with backstitch, using 1 thread of floss.
- For mounting instructions, see page 137.

BENJAMIN BUNNY BIB _____

Benjamin Bunny, a country squire with his pipe and walking stick, is perfect for a boy's bib. (It's always so much harder to find things for boys than girls.) You can add a padded "number one," which can be attached with Velcro to make a first birthday bib. Or you can appliqué Benjamin to the corner of a blanket or use him as the center of a quilt. Like Peter Rabbit, he is very versatile. You'll find Peter in needlepoint (or cross-stitch) on page 17.

MATERIALS

Calico fabric
Reverse print for pocket
Plain fabric for backing
Scraps of fabric for Benjamin
Cotton floss
Velcro
Quilt batting
Colors are: tan head and feet, white tail, yellow vest, lavender jacket, deep maroon cravat on a pale blue bib

ORDER OF WORKING

- Enlarge the bib from the graph pattern opposite.
- Trace each pattern piece from the full-size photo on heavy tracing paper. Cut the tracing paper into sections to form pattern pieces. Pin them down to fabric and trace around each one with a Trace Erase™ pen.
- Cut them out with ¼″ turnbacks.
- Stay stitch (running stitch) on the traced outline to make turnbacks clean cut.
- Snip turnbacks and finger press them back, using stay-stitch outlines as a guide. Do not turn back edges where one layer will overlap another. Leave them flat and sew the next layer in place on top.
- Trace the outline of Benjamin on the bib.
- Pin and stitch each piece in place, one by one. Start with legs, then vest, then jacket, then tail, then head, then collar, and, last, the gathered cravat. (Pad jacket with cot-

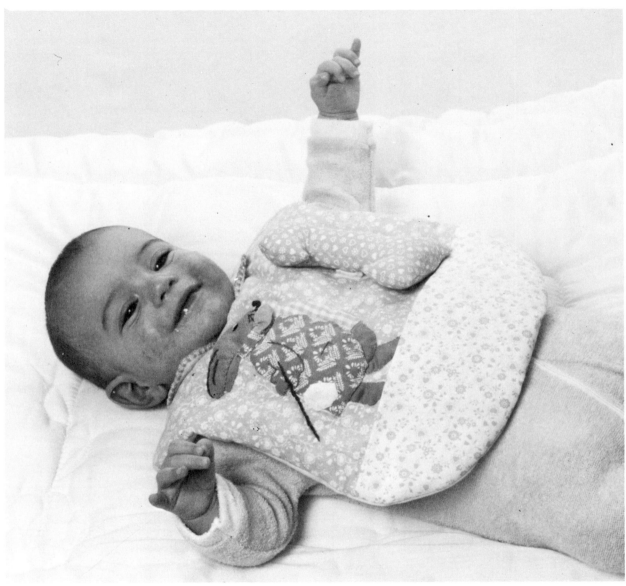

ton to raise it slightly.)
- Add embroidery details. Outline head and cane in stem stitch, pipe and eye in satin stitch.
- Make up bib from enlarged pattern opposite, or appliqué Benjamin Bunny on a ready-made bib.

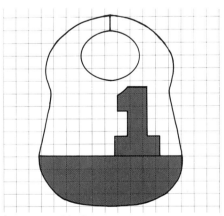

1 square = 1 inch

JIM HENSON'S MUPPETS™

Jim Henson's talents as a puppeteer were discovered early. As a senior in high school, he landed a job as a puppeteer with a local TV station, and while a freshman at the University of Maryland, he was offered his own show on WRC, the NBC affiliate in Washington, D.C. He asked Jane Nebel, a fellow art student (who later became his wife), to help, and together they produced "Sam and Friends." Jim nicknamed their troupe the Muppets™.

From the outset, there were some surprising things about the Muppets™. They didn't work on a stage or in a puppet theater. The performers worked freestanding in an open studio, watching the actual puppets on TV monitors. This let them have great control and gave their performances a remarkable feeling of freedom. This openness was enhanced by Jim's growing familiarity with the medium and his use of camera tricks and lens changes to exaggerate a sense of movement or an illusion of distance.

The success of "Sam and Friends" led to appearances on network television. The Muppets™ were frequent guests on the "Today," "Tonight," and "Ed Sullivan" shows, and Rowlf the Dog was the resident comedian on "The Jimmy Dean Show" for three years.

Jim Henson, shown in action at the left, is a relaxed, easy-going man. Lean, tall, and bearded, he controls a production calmly and quietly. Issuing suggestions rather than orders and listening to ideas from other members of his team, he gives as much leeway as possible to all the artists with whom he has surrounded himself. Teamwork is, in fact, the essence of Henson's varied enterprises.

Now that Kermit™ and Miss Piggy™ and their friends have become household words for people of all ages all over the world, they have taken their places beside such immortals as Winnie the Pooh and Peter Rabbit. Because they are puppets, made of fabric, you can have all kinds of fun with them in needlework, making anything from crochet finger puppets, as shown in these photos, to a bearskin rug. The next pages will give you a glimpse of the possibilities.

Text from *The Art of the Muppets*. A Muppet Press Book from Bantam Books. Muppet characters © Henson Associates, Inc. 1983 Muppets, Kermit the Frog, and Miss Piggy are trademarks of Henson Associates, Inc.

FOZZIE BEAR PUPPET

(Color Plate 12)

Fozzie is knitted in worsted yarn with a crocheted hat, ears, and tongue. First, knit the body and head, then pick up the stitches to join on the knitted arms and legs. Pad the head and body with a little cotton, sew on felt eyes and a pom-pom nose, tie a ribbon round his neck, and he's all ready to sit on your finger and charm your friends.

MATERIALS

Knitting worsted (1 oz. gold and small amounts of brown, pink and red)
½ yard ⅜″ white grosgrain ribbon
Pink pom-pom for nose
2 felt circles for eyes
Sequins
Cotton for stuffing
Sizes 2 and 3 double-pointed needles
Extra set of double-pointed needles or regular knitting needles to use as stitch holders
Size F crochet hook

Gauge: 6 sts = 1″ (stockinette stitch)

ORDER OF WORKING

As you knit, use a marker ring or piece of yarn to mark each round, moving it round by round.

Body

- Starting at the bottom of body on size 3 double-pointed needle, cast on 24 sts evenly spaced (8 sts on each of three needles). Work 12 rounds even.
- On the next round, increase 8 sts evenly spaced. Knit even for 14 rounds.
- Decrease by knitting together until you have 16 sts.
- Knit neck even for 3 rounds.

Head

- Round 1: Increase 11 sts evenly spaced around (27 sts).
- Round 2: Knit even for 8 rounds.
- Round 3: Bind off 12 sts (lower lip formed).
- Change to straight needles, picking up remaining 15 sts. Working in stockinette stitch (knit 1 row, purl 1 row), decrease 1 st at each end for 4 rows (7 sts left on the needle).
- Work even for 3 more rows and bind off (head and upper lip formed).
- Work 1 row single crochet (sc) evenly spaced around to finish mouth opening. *Caution:* Do not draw up crochet stitches too tightly.

Legs (see diagrams on facing page)

- Turn under 4 rows of the body at the bottom edge and hem with tiny stitches, using sewing thread that matches the yarn.
- Leave 10 sts for the back and pick up first 6 sts of the front with one size 2 double-pointed needle for front and leg and 6 sts again for the back of leg along fold line of the body. Knit even for 15 rows.
- End off by removing needles and weaving running thread through stitches with a tapestry needle and pull tightly. Finish off and cut yarn.
- Make the second leg exactly the same as the first, leaving 2 sts between each leg.

Arms (same as legs)

- Starting at the neck, count 2 rows down and pick up 6 sts for front of arm and 6 sts for the back. Knit even for 18 rounds.

- End off the same as the legs.
- Make second arm exactly as the first.

Ears (crochet)
- Chain 5 and work sc into second chain from hook and each chain across (4 sc).
- Row 2: Work even in sc.
- Row 3: Work 3 sc and bind off.

Mouth Lining
- With red yarn, cast on 10 sts. Knit 20 rows even and bind off.
- Attach to inside of the mouth, about ⅛″ in from edge, turning under the edges of the lining and easing it to fit as you sew.

Tongue
- With pink yarn, chain 5 and half sc in each chain all around (10 sc). Break off yarn.
- Sew tongue in mouth.
- Lightly stuff head and upper body.

Hat
- With brown yarn, start at crown of hat.
- Round 1: Chain 2, work 9 sc in second chain from hook. Mark the last stitch with a safety pin.
- Round 2: Sc in each sc around, increasing 3 sc evenly spaced.
- Round 3: To start forming the brim, work in back loop only, single crocheting in each sc round.
- Round 4: In back loop only, increase 3 sc evenly spaced.
- Round 5: In back loop only, increase 10 sc evenly spaced, then end off.
- Turn up brim on hat and sew hat to head.
- Tie ribbon around the neck and make a bow.
- Sew sequins to front of bow.
- Glue or sew pom-pom nose and felt eyes in place.
- Add detail to eyes with felt-tip pen.

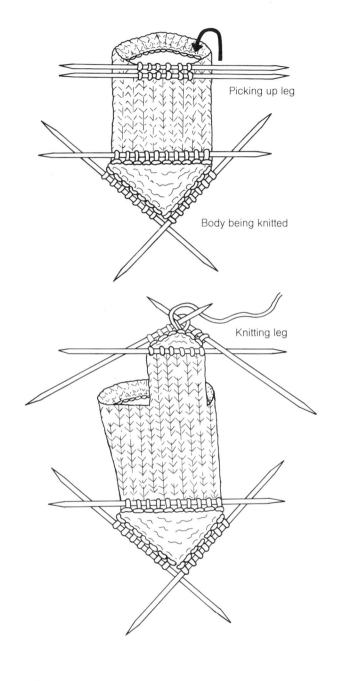

Picking up leg

Body being knitted

Knitting leg

MISS PIGGY™ PUPPET

(Color Plate 12)

To make the Miss Piggy™ crochet finger puppet, first establish the correct gauge by making a swatch 3–4″ square. Mark the end of each round with a safety pin or contrasting yarn, moving it forward as you go, so you do not lose your way.

MATERIALS

Small amounts of knitting worsted yarn in assorted colors
White pom-pom for hat
Beads for necklace
Rhinestone for ring
Small pieces of white and purple felt for eyes
Embroidery floss, stuffing, felt, pipe cleaners
Sizes 00 and 0 crochet hooks

Gauge: On 00 hook, 4 sts = 1″
       On 0 hook, 6 sts = 1″

ORDER OF WORKING

Head

- Begin at the center of the snout and continue to work in rounds for the face.
- Close the back of the head by working back and forth in rows slip-stitched to the sides of the face at each end (see diagrams).
- To complete, resume working in rounds for the neck and body.
- With peach yarn and a 00 hook, start at the center of the snout.
- Round 1: Chain (ch) 3, slip stitch: to join in ring. Work 6 single crochet (sc) in ring, ch 1.
- Round 2: Sc in back loops of round 1. Ch 1.
- Round 3: Work even in sc.
- Rounds 4–8: Continue to work in sc, increasing 4 sts evenly spaced over each round (26 sts). The face is now complete.
- Work 5 rows of sc over the next 13 sts for the back of the head, fastening the beginning and end of each row to the next re-maining st at either side of the face with a slip stitch.

Neck

- Resume working in rounds for neck.
- Round 1: Work 14 sc evenly spaced around neck opening.
- Round 2: Work even on 14 sc, join with slip stitch, ch 1, but do not turn.

Body

- Round 3: *Sc in each of next 7 sc, ch 2 (armhole), repeat from * once, join with slip stitch, ch 1, but do not turn.
- Rounds 4–7: Work 4 rounds even on 18 sc.
- Round 8: Increase 6 sc evenly spaced.
- Round 9: Work even on 24 sc.
- Round 10: Increase 4 sc evenly spaced.
- Round 11: Work even on 28 sc. End off.

Arms

- With peach yarn and an 0 hook, attach yarn at the armhole and work 8 sc around the armhole. Work 2 more rounds even on 8 sc.
- Change to lavender and work 7 rounds.
- Hold closed the opening at the end of the hand and make the fingers, working through both thicknesses.
- *Ch 2, sc in second ch from hook, slip stitch into the hand and repeat from * 2 times.
- Ch 3, sc in second and third ch from hook, slip stitch into the hand for the thumb.
- End off. (Make sure to work the thumb so that it points up when the arm is outstretched.) Fold pipecleaners in half and insert one in each arm.

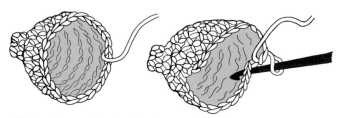

Making face and back of head

Ears, Hair, and Face

- With a 00 hook and peach yarn, ch 3, sc in second and third ch from hook, chain 1, turn.
- Work 2 rows even on 2 sc; work 2 sc together.
- End off.
- Sew the wider end of ear to top of head.
- To add yellow fringe for hair, cut yellow yarn into 5″ lengths, insert hook into the stitch at back of the head, and fold yarn over the end. Pull the yarn loop through the stitch with the hook. Pull the cut ends of yarn through the looped end and tug gently to form fringe knot. After fringing the hair area, trim ''hair'' and then fluff it by combing with a fine-tooth comb.
- Embroider red mouth.
- Cut eyes from felt, glue them in place, and outline with black embroidery thread.

Hat

- Use a 0 hook and lavender yarn.
- Round 1: Ch 2, work 5 sc in second ch from hook.
- Rounds 2–4: Increase 5 sc evenly spaced around.
- Round 5: Sc, ch 1 in each sc around.
- Round 6: 2 sc in each ch 1 evenly spaced around.
- Round 7: *Sc in next sc; sc, ch 1, and sc in next sc. Repeat from * around.
- End off.
- Sew pom-pom to center of hat and sew hat to head. Pull one ear through the hat and arrange hat over the other ear.

Dress and Bodice

- With a 00 hook and plum yarn, ch 20.
- Row 1: Sc in second ch from hook and each ch across.
- Row 2: Sc in back loop only of the next 4 sc; sc; work 7 double crochet (dc) in next sc; sc; sc in back loop only of next 5 sc; sc; work 7 dc in next sc; sc; sc in back loop only of next 4 sc.
- Row 3: Sc in back loop only of next 4 sc; ch 3; skip sc; 7 dc; sc; sc in back loop only of next 5 sc; ch 3; skip sc; 7 dc; sc; sc in back loop only of the next 4 sc.

- Row 4: Working in back loop only, increase 2 sc (20 sc).
- Row 5: Work even, join with slip stitch.

Skirt

- Work the skirt in rounds
- Round 1: *Sc; ch 2; skip 1; 3 dc, ch 1, 3 dc in the next sc; ch 2; skip 1. Repeat from * around; slip stitch in first sc.
- Round 2: Ch 1; sc in same st as slip stitch; *ch 3; 3 dc, ch 1, 3 dc in next ch 1 space from last row; ch 3; sc in next sc. Repeat from * around, ending with slip stitch in first sc.
- Round 3: Ch 1; sc in the same st as slip stitch; *ch 3; 4 dc, ch 1, 4 dc in ch 1 space from last row; ch 3; sc in next sc. Repeat from * around. Join. End off.
- Sew bodice back seam.
- String beads for necklace and sew rhinestone ''ring'' to the finger.

KERMIT™ PUPPET ____

(Color Plate 12)

Kermit™ is knitted and has felt feet and eyes. In each of the finger puppets, you can either pick up the stitches from the body to begin making the arms and legs or you can make them separately and join the parts by sewing.

MATERIALS

Knitting worsted (1 oz. green and small amounts of red, pink, and black)
4 pipe cleaners
Green felt for feet and collar
White felt for eyes
Small amount of stuffing
Size 2 double-pointed needles
Extra set of double-pointed needles or 4 regular needles to use as holders

Gauge: 5 sts = 1"

ORDER OF WORKING

- As you knit, use a marker ring or piece of yarn to mark each round, moving it round by round.

Body

- Starting at the bottom of the body with double-pointed needles, cast on 24 sts evenly spaced (8 sts on each of three needles). Knit 24 rounds even.
- Knit neck even for 3 rounds.

Mouth

- Leave 11 sts on double-pointed needle for back of head. With straight needles, pick up 9 sts for lower lip and work in stockinette stitch (knit 1 row, purl 1 row).
- Row 1: Knit row, decrease 1 st at each end (7 sts).
- Row 2: Purl row.
- Row 3: Knit row, decrease 1 st at each end (5 sts).
- Row 4: Purl row.
- Row 5: Bind off remaining 5 sts.

Head

- With 11 sts on straight needles, work 14 rows stockinette stitch.
- Next row: Bind off (upper lip formed).
- To finish, crochet 1 row of single crochet around edge of mouth.

Mouth Lining

- With red yarn, cast on 8 sts.
- Knit 16 rows even.
- Bind off.
- Attach to inside of mouth, about $\frac{1}{8}$" in from edge, turning under the edges of lining and easing to fit as you sew.

Legs

- Turn under 4 rows of body at bottom edge, and hem with tiny stitches using sewing thread that matches yarn.
- Leave 12 stitches for back and pick up first 5 sts of front with 1 double-pointed needle for front of leg and 5 sts again for back of leg along fold line of body.
- Knit even for 36 rows.
- End off by removing needles and weaving running thread through stitches with tapestry needle and pull tightly.
- Finish off and cut yarn.

Arms (same as legs)

- Starting at the bottom of the body, count 11 rows up and pick up 5 sts for front of arm and 5 sts for back.
- Knit even for 20 rounds.

Shaping the Hand

- Round 21: Place 2 sts on top side on holder for the thumb. Work on the remaining 8 sts for hand.
- Work 10 rounds even.
- Next round: Knit 2 together around.
- Cut yarn and draw through remaining 4 sts.
- Pull tight and sew hand shut.

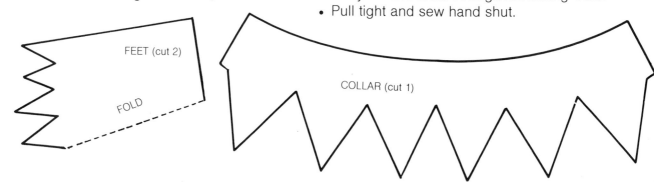

FEET (cut 2)

FOLD

COLLAR (cut 1)

Shaping the Thumb
- Work the thumb on 2 sts from holder, plus 2 sts picked up on the hand at base of thumb.
- Work 7 rounds on 4 sts.
- Next round: Work 2 together 2 times.
- Cut yarn and draw it through the loops and fasten off.
- Make the second arm exactly as the first.

Eyes
- Cut 2 half-inch circles from white felt.
- Gather around edge and draw up to form a ball and stuff tightly.
- Sew closed and sew to top of head. Embroider black detail on eyeball, using the photo as a guide.

Feet and Collar
- Insert a pipe cleaner into each leg and trim it to fit if necessary.
- Cut 2 feet from felt.
- With right sides together, fold foot in half and slip it over bottom of the leg with bottom of the leg even with the straight edge at top of foot.
- Sew across top of foot.
- Turn the foot right side out and glue shut.
- Cut out the collar and sew it in place.

GONZO PUPPET _____

(Color Plate 12)

Crochet Gonzo starting at the base of the body. Work up to loop stitch around the neck (beard) and beginning of the back of the head. Leave the head unfinished to work chin, and continue making the flap to fold back later inside the mouth. This runs on into the nose. When nose is complete, make tucks on either side of flap to form the mouth. Continue the back of head. The back of head and the nose are connected by sewing eyes and eyelids in place. Stiffen arms, legs, and trunk with pipe cleaners, then complete Gonzo with a knitted shirt front and a bow tie.

MATERIALS

Small amounts of knitting worsted (plum, purple, lavender, pink, red, white, gold, magenta, black)
3 pipe cleaners
Small amount of stuffing
Size F crochet hook
Size 2 knitting needles

Gauge: 5 sts = 1″

ORDER OF WORKING

Head and Body
- Start at bottom with plum yarn, chain (ch) 24. Join with slip stitch.
- Work single crochet (sc) in each ch around (through both loops).
- Working in back loops only, work 11 rounds sc.
- Next row: Decrease 6 sts (18 sts remain).

Head and Beard
- Using purple yarn, work loop stitch (see diagram on page 152) all around on next 2 rows. (Loops held over a pencil or a finger are the right size.) Leave the thread hanging.

Chin
- Using plum yarn, *sc in the next 8 sts.
- Next row: Sc, increasing 1 in each st (16 sts).
- Next 3 rows: Decrease 1 at each end of each row (14, 12, 10 sts remain)*.

Inside Mouth
- With pink yarn and working in back loops only, repeat between *'s, increasing instead of decreasing (16 sts formed).

Nose
- With purple yarn decrease 1 at each end of 5 rows sc (6 sts).
- Ch 3, slip stitch to join (9 sts).

- Next 4 rounds: Work round on 9 sts.
- Next 5 rounds: Decrease 1 st at end of each round (1 st remains).
- Loop through stitch to fasten off the nose.

Back of Head
- With purple yarn, work even in loop stitch for next 6 rows, and slip stitch onto face and mouth on either side as you go.
- Next 6 rows: Decrease 1 st at the end of each row (head completed).
- If desired, make side whiskers by adding 3 loop sts on either side of the nose.
- The back of head and top of nose are simply attached by eyes and eyelids.

Eyeball (make 2)
- With white yarn, ch 2.
- Round 1: Work 5 sc in second ch from hook.
- Round 2: Work 2 sc in each sc around.
- Round 3: Work even.
- Round 4: Work 2 together all around.
- Stuff eye and sew to top of head, referring to photo for placement. Sew black spot on each eye.

Eyelid (make 2)
- With gold yarn, ch 7.
- Work 6 rows of 6 sc each.
- Sew in place, overlapping the eye and attaching under loop stitch at the back of the head.

Tongue
- With pink yarn, ch 6.
- Sc in second ch from hook and next 3 ch, with 3 sc in last ch and 4 sc along other side of ch.
- Sew tongue into mouth.

Legs (make 2)
- With plum yarn, work 10 sc, 5 into the front loops of base of body, 5 into the back loops.
- Next 12 rows: Work even in sc.
- Change to black yarn and decrease 2 sc.

- Next 5 rows: Work even.
- With blunt tapestry needle, weave running thread through and draw up tightly. Break yarn.

Arms (make 2)
- With plum yarn, work 8 sc evenly spaced around armhole.
- Work 6 rounds even on 8 sc.
- Change to white yarn and increase 4 sts evenly spaced.
- Work one more round with white.
- Change to purple yarn and work 3 rounds of loop stitch.
- Gather the tip of the hand and sew shut. Insert a piece of pipe cleaner into each arm.

Shirt Front
- With white yarn, cast on 16 sts.
- Work in stockinette stitch, decreasing 1 st at each end of the needle every other row until there are 2 sts left.
- Purl 1 row and bind off.
- Sew to front, hiding top edge under chin whiskers.
- Work 4 French knots with black for buttons.

Tie
- With magenta yarn, chain 6.
- Sc in second ch from hook and each of next 3 ch, with 3 sc in last ch, 4 sc along other side of ch, and 3 sc in first ch.
- Hold tie in place on shirt front and sew tightly around middle to form bow.

Lapels (make 2)
- With magenta yarn, ch 13.
- Sc in second ch from hook and each remaining ch.
- Ch 3 and turn.
- Double crochet (dc) in first and second sts, slip stitch in next st, ch 2, dc in same stitch as slip stitch, half double-crochet in next stitch, sc in next stitch, and slip stitch in next stitch.
- Sew along the edge of the shirt.

KERMIT™ SOCK APPLIQUÉS _____

(*Color Plate 17*)

Embroidered Kermit™ patches can be stitched to knee socks, sweat shirts, pants, and even sneakers.

MATERIALS

Cotton floss
#4 embroidery needle
Small piece of transparent organdy or Trace Erase™ fabric
Transparent-drying glue

ORDER OF WORKING

- Using a fine-point permanent marker or Trace Erase™ pen, trace the outline of Kermit™ on organdy or a double layer of Trace Erase™ fabric.
- With 2 strands of floss, stitch eyes, mouth, and collar in satin stitch and the face with long and short stitch (refer to Color Plate 17). Define the top edge of mouth with green stem stitch and complete eyes with black straight stitches topped with French knots.
- Paint a thin coat of transparent-drying glue over reverse side of appliqué, making sure to coat it completely, especially at the edges. Let dry. Carefully cut around the appliqué, close to edge of stitching. (Glue will hold edges and stop fraying without turnbacks.)
- Stitch appliqués in place as desired.

MUPPETS™ PUPPETS PANEL _____

(Color Plate 18)

The Muppets™ come to life when you make this 22 × 32″ panel in three-dimensional embroidery, using all the scraps from your workbasket. Suitable fabrics can express each character perfectly: for instance, brown terry toweling for Rowlf, light nylon stockings for the soft sculpture faces of Statler and Waldorf, satin for Miss Piggy™, and felt for Kermit™.

MATERIALS

22″ × 32″ stretcher strips
1 yard light blue cotton fabric
¼ yard medium blue cotton fabric
Assorted remnants of felt, satin, terry, and yarns
10″ × 20″ square of sheer pink or beige single-knit or hosiery fabric
Poly-fiberfill
Poly-quilt batting
Assorted bits of costume jewelry, feathers, sequins, ribbons, and trimmings
Cotton floss
Cardboard

ORDER OF WORKING

- Enlarge patterns on pages 54–55 and 153–157.
- Stretch light blue cotton fabric over stretcher strips.
- With Trace Erase™ pen, trace outlines of characters on fabric. *Note:* The darker blue section at the bottom of panel is 6″ high. Begin working on characters in the background, adding or layering new characters and working foreground characters last.
- Refer to the photo here and Color Plate 18 for colors and suggested ideas for embellishments, clothing textures, and so on.

All characters are worked in the same basic way:

- Use a Trace Erase™ pen to trace outlines of each section of a character on appropriate fabric.

- Turnings on nonraveling fabrics, such as felt, are unnecessary. Woven fabrics do require turnings, however, so add ¼ to ⅜". Snip curved turnbacks so they will lie smoothly.
- Appliqué each area to the panel with tiny stitches at right angles to the edge. Stuff small bits of fiberfill under each area as you sew it down to give it dimension. You can quilt through all layers to define arms, ears, hair curls, etc.
- In some instances it may be easier to appliqué smaller pieces to larger ones, then appliqué the larger pieces in place. (For example, add eyes and nose to face, then add face to the panel.) The same is true for embroidered features—do the embroidery, then appliqué face to the panel.
- To make a soft sculpture face, draw the face on a piece of single-knit fabric, leaving several inches of extra fabric all around.
- Place about a handful of fiberfill behind the traced face and draw excess fabric together at back with running stitches.
- Sculpt by stitching around shapes with a running stitch. You can control the size and shape by varying the amount of fiberfill you pick up with your needle and how tightly you draw up the thread.
- Apply cheek or mouth color with blushing rouge or felt-tipped markers.

Kermit™
- Kermit's head is made first and then sewn in place.
- Trace full-size patterns on page 53 on felt. You must add seam allowances for head and mouthpiece.
- Appliqué tongue and throat to red mouthpiece.
- Sew top and bottom head seams, then stitch mouth into opening.
- Cut a piece of cardboard the shape of mouthpiece but about ¼" smaller all around, and crease it on fold line. Glue in place behind the mouth to stiffen it.
- Stuff head with fiberfill.
- Embroider or appliqué pupils on eyes. Make running stitches around edges of eyes. Draw up, stuff with fiberfill, and sew in position on either side of head.
- Sew bottom of head in a flat seam from side to side. Stitch in position on top of appliquéd body.

FINISHING
- Complete the Muppets™ appliqué except for parts that overlap the darker blue section at the bottom.
- Cut the darker blue fabric 9 x 36" and stitch on long edge in place at base of characters with a 6 x 32" piece of quilt batting layered under it. Stretch bottom and sides of fabric over stretcher strips and staple them in place. Quilt horizontal rows 1" apart through all layers.
- Complete appliqué sections that overlap the dark blue section.

How to appliqué in layers

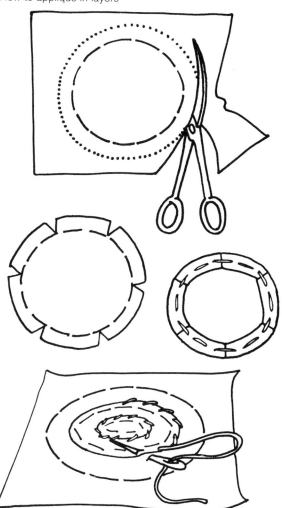

52

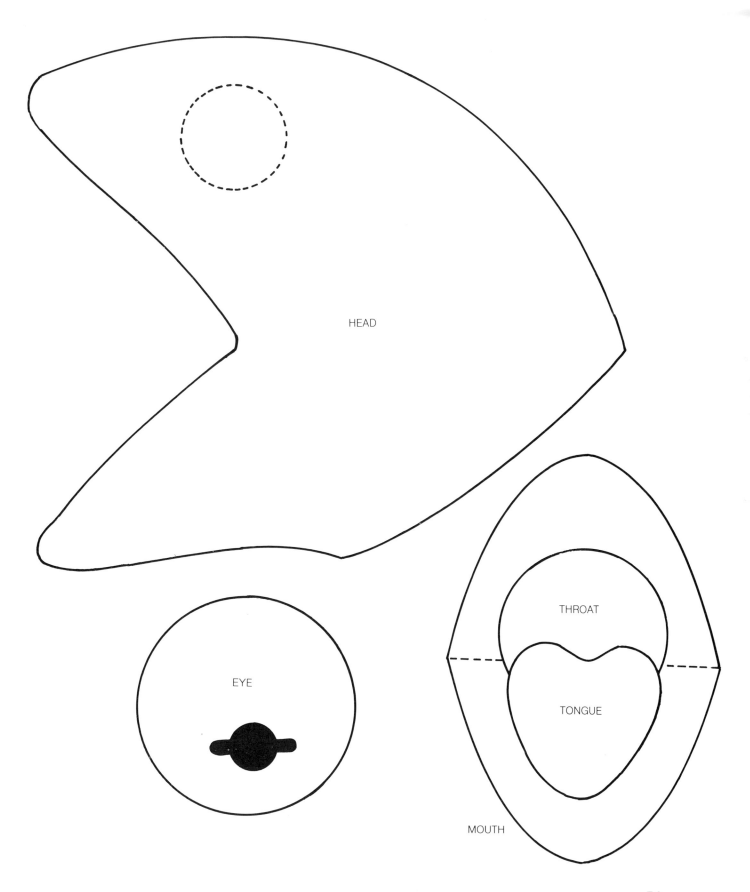

HEAD

EYE

THROAT

TONGUE

MOUTH

53

54

MISS PIGGY™ PILLOW _____

(Color Plates 13 and 14)

Miss Piggy™ of the Muppets™ is a femme fatale in a maribou-edged robe. Wearing a pearl necklace, lying on a blue satin pillow with lacy frill, she is bound to be a conversation piece wherever she goes, especially when you read her succinct message at the back: "You can never be too rich or too thin."

MATERIALS

1 yard champagne satin
½ yard gold satin
⅓ yard blue satin
¼ yard flesh satin
Scrap of lavender satin
Trace Erase™ pen
1½ yards white lace about 2½" wide
Embroidery floss
Rhinestone button
1 yard feather boa
1 strand costume pearls

Small amount quilt batting
Fiberfill

ORDER OF WORKING

- Enlarge patterns (1 square = 1") on page 59. *Note:* No seam allowances have been added.
- With Trace Erase™ pen, trace, but do not cut out, the entire outline of the front and back sections on two 18 × 36" rectangles of champagne satin.
- Mount the front rectangle in an embroidery frame.
- Trace the actual-size patterns on page 58 for the hair, face, and glove pieces on appropriate colors (refer to Color Plate 13).
- Appliqué face first (embroidery features will be added later).
- Appliqué hair in position with a layer of batting sandwiched behind hair section. With matching thread, quilt the curls into

56

hair along the dotted lines.

- Work the face features with three threads of cotton floss as follows:

Tongue	wine red satin stitch
Nose	gold stem stitch
Eyelids	lavender satin stitch
Pupils	black vertical satin stitch with white highlights
Iris	blue satin stitch (starry-eyed look is achieved by working spaced black stitches radiating around pupil on top of blue)
White of eye	satin stitch
Eyelashes	black straight stitches around eye (as in chart and photo)

- Enlarge and transfer front blue pillow sections and appliqué in place.
- Appliqué lavender glove, pad, and quilt with matching thread. Stitch ring in place.
- Mount the back rectangle of satin in an embroidery frame.
- Work the lettering on back rectangle in stem stitch, using 6 threads of blue floss.
- Appliqué, pad, and quilt hair for back in gold satin as was done for front hair.
- Trace two of the ear pattern on page 58 and stitch together with right sides facing. Stuff with batting and pleat the front to be ready for insertion in seam.
- Enlarge and transfer the back pillow section and appliqué in place.
- Stitch the back and front rectangles together, inserting ears and lace frill in seam.
- Pad the pillow. Stitch the additional lace frill front and back from the edge across the pillow section as marked by X's in the diagram.
- On the dotted lines indicated, stitch a double line of maribou with couching stitches in white cotton floss.
- Stitch the pearl necklace in place as the finishing touch.

HAND (cut 1)

EAR (cut 4)

58

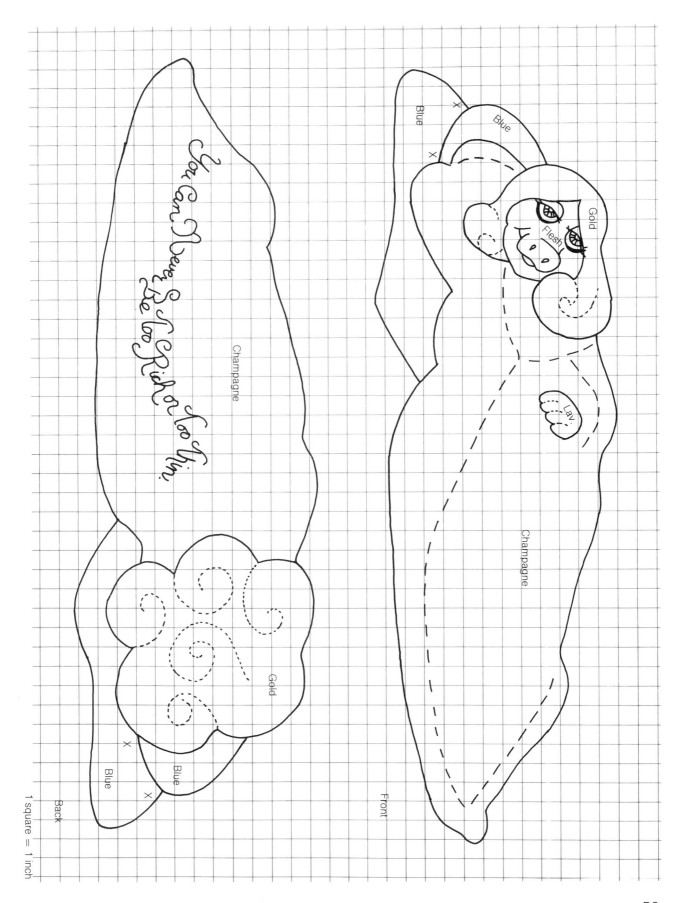

You Can Never Be Too Rich or Too Thin.

Champagne

Blue

Blue

Gold

Flesh

Lav.

Champagne

Gold

Blue

Blue

Back

Front

1 square = 1 inch

59

FOZZIE BEAR RUG

(Color Plate 15)

Fozzie Bear is worked in latch hook in a combination of longer rya and shorter precut yarns to give texture and dimension. He can also be worked in cross-stitch or needlepoint, counting from the graphs on pages 62–63.

MATERIALS

1¼ yards (3.75 mesh) rug canvas
Latch hook
Precut latch-hook yarn
Precut latch-hook rya yarn
Rug binding

ORDER OF WORKING

- Tape edges of canvas to prevent raveling.
- Finished bear measures approx. 22 × 44". Be sure to leave at least 2" of unworked canvas all around.
- Follow latch-hook technique, as explained below, working knots over parallel threads, *not* twisted threads. Work across row by row counting out the pattern from the graph and referring to Color Plate 15. Work across the entire row, changing colors as necessary. Begin with the bottom row and work each new row above the one just finished. The shaded areas of the graph are worked with regular length precut latch-hook yarn. The unshaded areas are worked with rya length precut latch-hook yarn.

MOUNTING AND FINISHING

- Trim canvas to within 1" of pile all around.
- Fold canvas to back and whip stitch, turning it in place with heavy thread. Slash the canvas as necessary to make curved areas lie flat.
- Whip stitch one edge of rug binding around outside edge of rug (on the turning edge). Then sew the inside edge of binding to the underside of canvas, easing in fullness as necessary to make it lie flat.

Latch Hooking

1. Fold the yarn over the shaft of the hook, making sure the ends of the yarn are even.
2. Hold on to the yarn as you insert the head of the hook under the canvas thread and up into the hole immediately above.
3. Pull the hook back toward you. The latch will open, allowing you to lay the two ends of the yarn between the latch and the hook. Draw the hook toward you and the latch will close around both ends of the yarn. Release the yarn. Continue to pull the latch through the canvas.
4. Give a gentle tug to the ends to secure them.

Yarn Colors: Rya

Body: Medium orange
Body outlines: Dark orange

Yarn Colors: Latch Hook

Eyebrows, ear accents, eyelashes, main hat: Medium brown
Hat accents: Dark brown
Eyes: Black, white, with magenta above eyelashes
Nose: Hot pink
Mouth: Maroon, red, light pink
Dots on tie: Hot pink inside, light pink outside
Bow tie: White with gray outlines

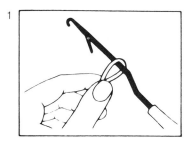
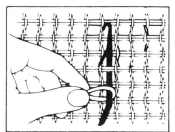
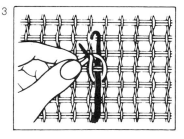
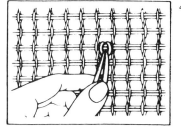

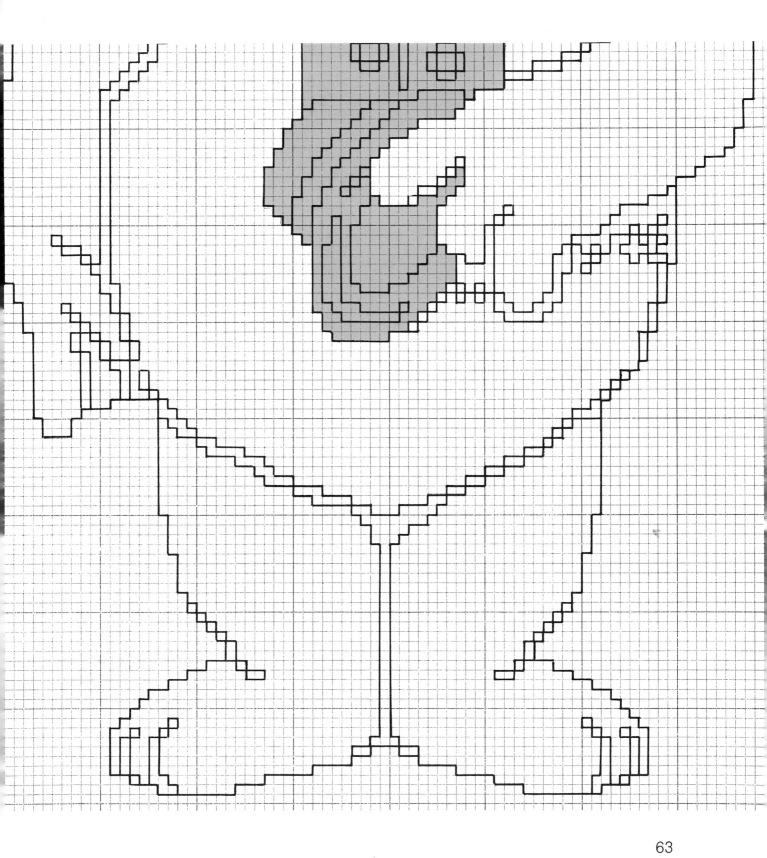

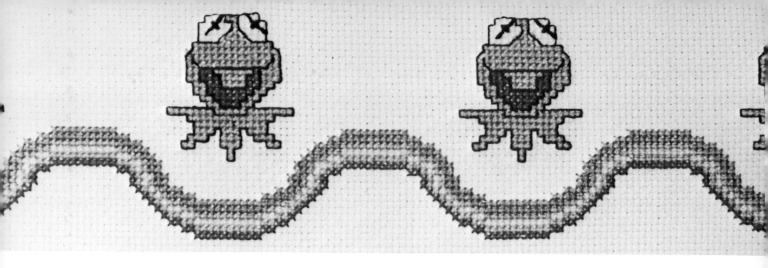

KERMIT™ CROSS-STITCH

(Color Plate 16)

Colorful cross-stitch Kermits™ smiling between the rainbows could be used to decorate anything from a tea towel, tissue box, book cover, or a recipe file to a bib or the yoke of a child's dress.

MATERIALS

15 × 26" Cream # 14 Aida cloth
Cotton floss
20 tapestry needle

ORDER OF WORKING

- Separate the 6-strand floss and work the motifs in cross-stitch with 3 strands, following the graph and Color Plate 16.

- Outline Kermit in back stitch with a single strand of black floss, the "eye centers" with 3 strands.

FINISHING A TOWEL

- Turn edges ¼", then 1" toward back.
- Slip stitch in place.

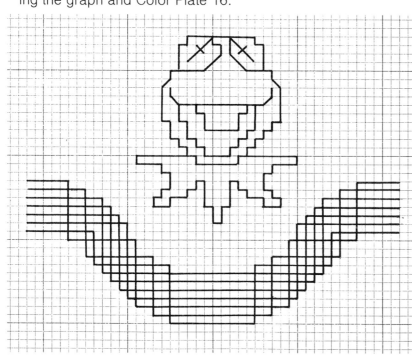

Plate 12. "MUPPETS™" crocheted hand puppets (pages 42–48). Muppet Characters © Henson Associates, Inc. 1983.

13.

You Can Never Be Too Rich or Too Thin.

14.

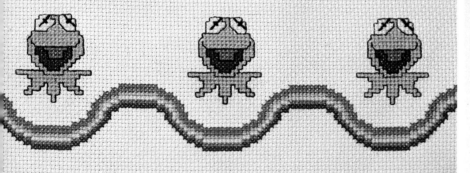

16.

Plate 13. "YOU CAN NEVER BE TOO RICH OR TOO THIN" Miss Piggy™ cushion (page 56).

Plate 14. Back view of Miss Piggy™ cushion (Plate 13).

Plate 15. "FOZZIE BEAR" latch-hook rug (page 61).

Plate 16. "KERMIT™" cross-stitch design (page 64).

15.

Plate 17.   ''KERMIT™'' appliqué socks (page 49).

Plate 18.   ''MUPPETS™'' puppets panel (page 51).

16.

17.

8.

JEAN DE BRUNHOFF

The stories of Babar the Elephant and his wife, Queen Celeste, and all his friends and relations have been favorites for so long—since the early 1930s, in fact—that everyone asks with astonishment, "The author is still alive?" The answer is told in Laurent de Brunhoff's words.

"My childhood was filled with painting, music, and books. My grandfather published the superb programs of Diaghilev's Ballets Russes while my uncles published magazines such as *Vogue, VU,* and *Le Jardin des Modes.* My mother was a pianist, and my father, Jean de Brunhoff, was a painter in the impressionist tradition.

"In 1930 my mother told my brother and me a story about a little elephant. We enjoyed it so much that we told it to my father, who then developed the plot to make a book for us. We loved it. This home-made Story of Babar was also very successful with the adults in the family, particularly with my uncles, the magazine publishers. And in 1931 *The Story of Babar* was published in hardcover by Le Jardin des Modes.

"The book was so well received and Jean de Brunhoff enjoyed his new career as author/illustrator so much that he immediately began other books about Babar. When my father died in 1937 he had written and illustrated seven books altogether. Jean de Brunhoff's last two books, which were published after his death, were not completely finished and I was asked to color a few of

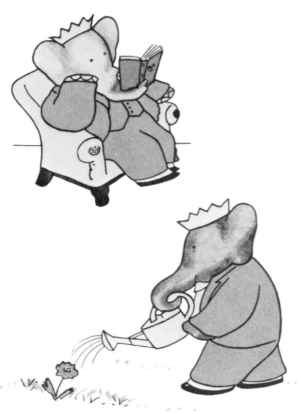

Drawings from *Babar and His Children,* © 1938, 1966 Random House, Inc. Reprinted with permission.

Drawing from *Babar's French Lessons*,
© 1963 Random House, Inc.
Reprinted with permission.

those pages. I was twelve at the time, and I already wanted to be a painter. I drew elephants everywhere, of course.

"After World War II, I was myself a painter, but in the abstract tradition, and living in a studio in Montparnasse when I decided to carry on the adventures of Babar. I worked to maintain the great faithfulness in the drawings. It would have been senseless to continue Babar without respecting his already established style and spirit. So in 1946 I published *Babar and That Rascal Arthur.* I featured Arthur because I identified most easily with him. Jean de Brunhoff had taken inspiration from his own family in detailing the adventures of Babar. When I published my first book I was barely 21, with no family of my own. I felt I had a lot in common with teenage Arthur.

"For a long time the general public remained unaware of the death of my father and thought that the interruption of the *Babar* series was due to the war. I often met people who were very surprised to see that the author of Babar was such a young man. They expected me to have a long white beard. Now I am older than my father ever was and sometimes that is an eerie feeling. I've done so many books that I no longer have to *think* of being faithful to the tradition anymore. Babar appears at the tip of my pencil as if I had invented this character myself.

"People sometimes ask me in astonishment if I only work on children's books. It is true that I enjoy doing other kinds of drawing, but basically I love to draw for children. They accept, even demand, the greatest freedom in fantasy; their minds are not burdened by preconceptions . . . not yet. They are able to enjoy wonder, laughter, and tears more freely than adults."

The panel opposite and the robe on page 79 just begin to show the imaginative ideas that these simply classic stories can inspire.

66

BABAR AND CELESTE

(Color Plate 19)

Celeste is made identically to Babar except that the jacket, made in white and embroidered with multicolored French knots for her, is worn backward. Tack the opening of her jacket together at the back of the neck.

Begin working the bodies from the necks down. Work the legs at the base of the body. Make the head separately, starting at the end of the trunk, and sew it to the top of the body. Make two arms and sew them in place. Complete Babar and Celeste with jackets and crowns.

MATERIALS

Sizes F and G crochet hooks
Knitting worsted: 30 yards green, 5 yards black, 15 yards white, 1½ yards red, 3 yards yellow, and 20 yards gray.
Gauge: Size F   9 sts = 2″, 4 rows = 1″
        Size G   4 sts = 1″, 4 rows = 1″

ORDER OF WORKING

- Chain (ch) 1 and turn at end of every row unless directed otherwise.

- Rounds are not joined; mark the beginning of each round with a safety pin.
- To change colors, draw up loop with first color and work off with second color. Tie knot on inside of work.
- To keep work neat, leave approximately 8″ tails at ends of pieces for sewing. Crochet over or weave in other loose ends as you work.

Body

- Starting at neck edge, with F hook and white yarn, ch 15 and join with slip stitch to form a ring.
- Round 1: Ch 1, single crochet (sc) in same ch as slip stitch, sc in each remaining ch around (15 sc).
- Round 2: Increase in every fifth sc around (18 sc).
- Round 3: Increase in every sixth sc around (21 sc). Change to green yarn.
- Round 4: Increase in every seventh sc around (24 sc).
- Round 5: Work even on 24 sts.
- Round 6: * Sc in next 4 sc, decrease 1 sc, repeat from * around (20 sc).

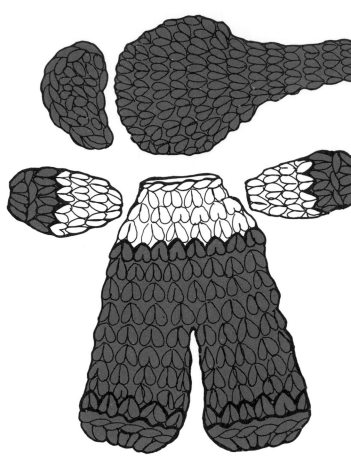

First Leg

- Slip stitch in next sc, ch 3, skip next 9 sc, slip stitch in next sc for leg opening; ch 1 but do not turn.
- Round 1: Sc in same st as slip stitch and in each of next 9 sc, sc in each of 3 ch sts (13 sc).
- Rounds 2–5: Work even on 13 sc, then change to white yarn.
- Round 6: Mark front of leg, sc in each sc around, increase 2 sc at front of leg. Change to black yarn.

- Round 7: Sc in each sc around, increasing 3 sc at front of leg.
- Round 8: *Working in back loop only, work 2 sts together around (9 sts). Break off.

Second Leg

- Round 1: Attach yarn at leg opening with sc in same sc as slip stitch, sc in each of next 9 sc, sc in each of 3 ch sts (13 sc).
- Rounds 2–8: Work same as first leg.

Bow tie

- With red yarn and F hook, ch 3, work 2 half double-crochet (hdc) in third ch from hook. Break off yarn. Attach yarn in same third ch as above and work ch 2, 2 hdc and break off.
- Sew bow tie to front of shirt and stuff body.

Head

- Starting at end of trunk, ch 2 with gray yarn and F hook.
- Round 1: Work 5 sc in second ch from hook.
- Rounds 2–4: Work even on 5 sc.
- Round 5: Increase 1 sc.
- Round 6: Work even on 6 sc.
- Rounds 7–9: Increase 1 sc on each round (9 sc).
- Round 10: Increase in every third sc around (12 sc).
- Round 11: Increase in every second sc around (18 sc).
- Round 12: Increase 2 sc evenly spaced (20 sc).
- Round 13: Increase in every fifth sc around (24 sc).

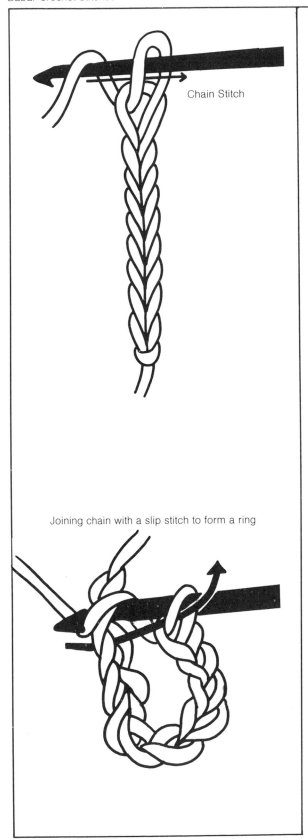

Chain Stitch

Joining chain with a slip stitch to form a ring

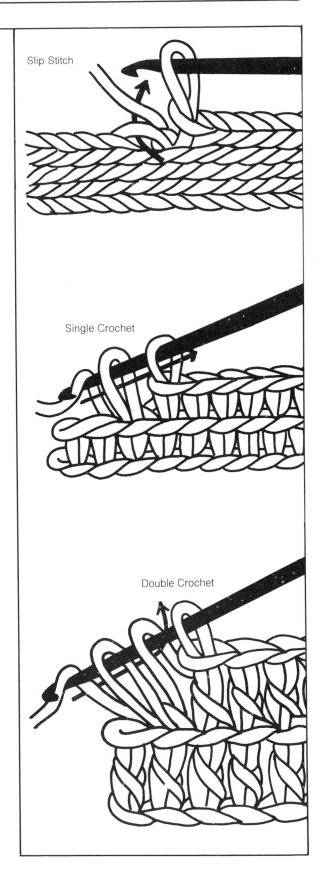

Slip Stitch

Single Crochet

Double Crochet

- Round 14: Work even on 24 sc.
- Round 15: *Sc in each of next 2 sc, decrease 1 sc, repeat from * around (18 sc).
- Round 16: *Sc in next sc, decrease 1 sc, repeat from * around (12 sc). Stuff the head.
- Round 17: Work 2 sts together all around. Break off.
- Sew the opening closed and sew the head to body. Sew foot openings closed.

Ears
- For right ear, ch 4 with gray yarn and F hook.
- Row 1: Sc in second ch from hook, sc in next ch, 3 sc in last ch.
- Row 2: Work 2 sc in each of next 3 sc, slip stitch in next sc, 2 sc in next sc, break off.
- For left ear, ch 4.
- Row 1: Work 3 sc in second ch from hook, work 1 sc in each of next 2 ch.
- Row 2: 2 sc in next sc; slip stitch in next sc; 2 sc in each of next 3 sc. Break off.
- Sew ears to sides of head with wider part of ear near top of head.

Tusks (make 2)
- With F hook and white yarn, ch 3, slip stitch in second ch from hook, sc in next ch. Break off.
- Sew tusks to sides of face near base of trunk.

Arms (make 2)
- With gray yarn, and F hook, ch 2.
- Round 1: Work 8 sc in second ch from hook.
- Round 2: Working in back loop only, 1 sc in each sc around. Change to white yarn.
- Rounds 3–8: With white yarn, work even on 8 sc.
- Stuff arm, sew opening shut, and sew to side of body.

Crown
- With F hook and yellow yarn, ch 18, join with slip stitch to form ring.

- Round 1: Slip stitch counts as first st, sc in next ch, slip stitch in next ch, repeat slip stitch, sc, slip stitch 5 more times.
- Round 2: *Slip stitch in next stitch (slip stitch of previous row); sc, ch 1, sc in next sc; slip stitch in next slip stitch; repeat from * around.
- Sew crown to top of head. With black yarn, embroider two eyes and a small smile for the mouth.

Jacket
- With G hook and green yarn, ch 9.
- Row 1: Work sc in second ch from hook and each ch across.
- Row 2: Work even on 8 sc (back yoke).
- Row 3: Sc in first 2 sc.
- Row 4: Work even on 2 sc.
- Row 5: Sc in each sc, ch 3, turn.
- Row 6: Sc in second and third ch from hook and in each sc (4 sc).
- Row 7: Work even on 4 sc, break yarn (left front).
- Row 8: Attach yarn in last sc of row 2; work sc in last sc of row 2.
- Rows 9–11: Repeat rows 4–6.
- Row 12: Repeat row 7, but do not break yarn (right front), ch 1, turn.
- Row 13: Sc in each of next 4 sc, ch 4, work 8 sc across the opposite side of starting ch on the back yoke, ch 4, sc across 4 sc on left front (armholes formed).
- Row 14: Work 1 sc in each sc and ch of previous row (24 sc).
- Row 15: Increase 2 sc evenly spaced.
- Row 16: Work even on 26 sc. Break off.
- For sleeves, attach yarn at the armhole. Work 13 sc evenly spaced around. Work even for 3 more rounds.
- For collar, attach yarn at the front of the neck edge and work 13 sc evenly spaced across the neck. In next row, work even on 13 sc.
- To finish the jacket, weave in loose ends and lightly steam, folding back collar and lapels.

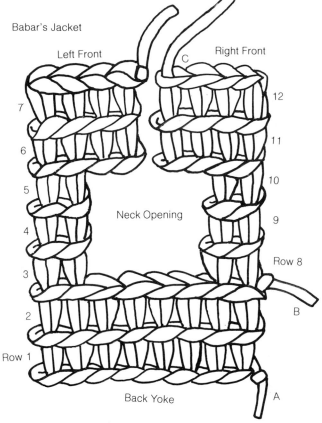

Babar's Jacket

Left Front   Right Front

7   12

6   11

5   10

Neck Opening

4   9

3   Row 8

2   B

Row 1

Back Yoke   A

A = Begin work

B = Join yarn for row 8

C = Begin row 13

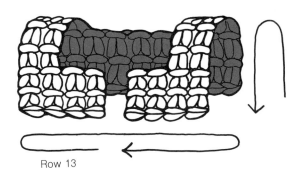

Row 13

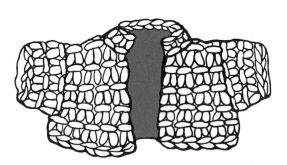

POM

Begin working Pom at the body from the neck down. Work the legs at the base of the body. Then make the head separately, starting at the end of the trunk. Sew the finished head to the top of the body. Make arms and two ears and sew them in place. Complete it with the shirt.

MATERIALS

Knitted worsted: 20 yards gray, 8 yards blue, 8 yards white, a small length of black for eyes and mouth
Sizes D and F aluminum crochet hooks
Stuffing

Gauge: D hook   5 sts = 1", 5 rows = 1"
       F hook   9 sts = 2", 4 rows = 1"
(Finished elephant is about 3½" tall.)

ORDER OF WORKING

Body

- Starting at neck edge with gray yarn and a D hook, ch 12 and join with slip stitch to form a ring.
- Round 1: Ch 1, sc in same ch as slip stitch, sc in each remaining ch around (12 sc).
- Round 2: Increase in every fourth sc around (15 sc).
- Round 3: With blue yarn, increase in every fifth sc around (18 sc).
- Round 4: Increase in every sixth sc around (21 sc).
- Round 5: *Sc in next 5 sc, decrease 1 sc, repeat from * around.

First Leg

- Slip stitch in next sc, ch 2, skip next 8 sc, slip stitch in next sc for leg opening, ch 1 but do not turn.
- Round 1: Sc in same st as slip stitch and in each of next 8 sc, sc in each of 2 ch sts (11 sc).
- Round 2: With gray yarn and working in

back loop only, sc in each sc around.

- Round 3: Work even on 11 sc. Mark front of leg.
- Round 4: Sc in each sc around, increasing 2 sc at front of leg.
- Round 5: With blue yarn, sc in each sc around, increasing 3 sc at front of leg (16 sc).
- Round 6: Working in back loop only, work 2 sts together all around (8 sts). Break off.

Second Leg

- Round 1: Attach blue yarn at leg opening with sc in same sc as slip stitch, sc in each of next 8 sc, sc in each of 2 ch sts (11 sc).
- Rounds 2–6: Work the same as the first leg.
- Stuff the body.

Head

- Starting at end of trunk with gray yarn and a D hook, ch 2.
- Round 1: Work 5 sc in second ch from hook.
- Rounds 2–4: Work even on 5 sc.
- Round 5: Increase 1 sc.
- Round 6: Work even on 6 sc.
- Round 7: Increase 2 sc evenly spaced.
- Round 8: Increase in every second sc around (12 sc).
- Round 9: Increase in every third sc around (16 sc).
- Round 10: Increase 2 sc evenly spaced.
- Round 11: Work even on 18 sc.
- Round 12: *Sc in next sc, decrease 1, repeat from * around. Stuff the head.
- Round 13: Work 2 sts together all around. Fasten off.
- Sew the opening closed and sew head to body. Sew feet closed.
- With black yarn, embroider two eyes and a small smile.

Ears

- For left ear, with gray yarn and a D hook, ch 3.

- Row 1: 3 sc in second ch from hook, 1 sc in next ch.
- Row 2: 2 sc in first sc, slip stitch in next sc, 2 sc in each of next 2 sc. Break off.
- For right ear, ch 3.
- Row 1: Sc in second ch from hook, 3 sc in next ch.
- Row 2: 2 sc in each of next 2 sc, slip stitch in next sc, 2 sc in next sc.
- Sew ears to sides of head with wider part of ear near top of head.

Arms (make 2)

- With gray yarn and a D hook, ch 6.
- Work 5 rows of 5 sc each row. Break off.
- Fold arm in half lengthwise and sew together. Sew arms to sides of body.

Shirt

- With an F hook and white yarn, ch 7.
- Row 1: Sc in second ch from hook and each remaining ch.
- Row 2: Work even on 6 sc.
- Row 3: Sc in each of next 2 sc.
- Row 4: Work even on 2 sc. Break off.
- Row 5: Attach yarn in the last sc on row 2, sc in last and next to last sc on row 2.
- Row 6: Work even on 2 sc.
- Row 7: Sc in each of next 2 sc, ch 2, sc in 2 sc from row 4 (neck opening formed).
- Row 8: Sc in each sc and ch (6 sc).
- Row 9: Work even on 6 sc.
- Row 10: Sc in each of next 6 sc, ch 3, work 6 sc across opposite side of starting ch, ch 3, join with slip stitch to first sc, ch 1 but do not turn.
- To form armholes, work 1 sc in each sc and ch around (18 sc). In next row, increase 2 sc evenly spaced, slip stitch in last sc. Break off.

Sleeves

- Work 12 sc evenly spaced around the armhole. Work 1 round, decreasing 2 sc under arm, slip stitch in last sc. Break off.
- Weave in loose ends.

BABAR IN A BALLOON WALL HANGING

(Color Plate 19)

The crocheted Babars (pages 67–72) descending in a balloon can be taken out of their knitted basket and returned to the wall when not in use.

MATERIALS

Two 17″ and two 22″ Artists' stretcher strips
⅔ yard blue cotton (such as sail cloth)

3" square black felt
12" × 18" yellow felt
Yellow cotton floss
Few yards white worsted-weight yarn
1 oz. cream rug and craft yarn
Size 7 knitting needles or the size required to obtain the correct gauge (4 sts = 1" garter stitch)
Polyester quilt batting
2⅓ yards red grosgrain ribbon (⅞" wide)
⅔ yard muslin

ORDER OF WORKING

- Enlarge balloon pattern on page 75.
- Stretch muslin, one layer of batting, then blue fabric over stretcher strips. Staple or tack it in place.
- Using tailor's chalk or a Trace Erase™ pen, lightly trace guidelines for placement of the basket and balloon on blue fabric.
- Cut balloon out of yellow felt, allowing 1" extra along the straight edges at top and sides of panel—but not along the curved edge—for turning over the stretcher strips. Cut a piece of batting the same shape but about ¼" smaller all around.
- Position batting and then felt over blue fabric and baste. Buttonhole stitch (¼" apart, with 6 strands floss) along the curved edge (see diagram this page). Staple extra 1" of felt at top and sides to edges of stretcher strips.
- With white yarn make long straight stitches from balloon to inside of basket position (see diagram this page and photo).
- Use cream rug and craft yarn to make basket. Cast on 20 st. Working entirely in garter stitch, increase 1 st each side every ¾" until you have 28 sts. Work even until total length from beginning is 3¾".
- Bind off. With matching thread, sew bottom and sides to panel along placement lines (see diagram this page). With white yarn make a twisted cord rope (page 152).
- Trace full-size anchor pattern (page 75) on

74

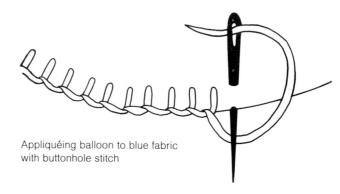

Appliquéing balloon to blue fabric with buttonhole stitch

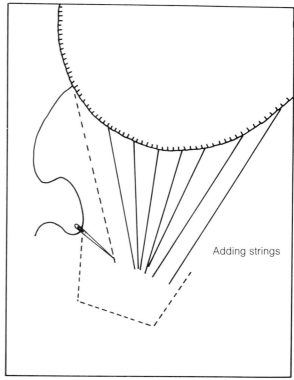

Adding strings

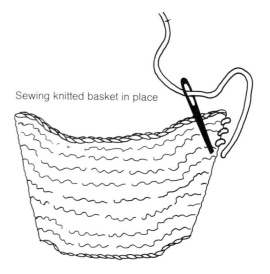

Sewing knitted basket in place

black felt and cut out. Cut a ⅛ × ¾″ strip of black felt for rope holder.

- Loop one end of the rope through the anchor and catch stitch.
- Referring to photo, stitch bottom of black "rope holder" in place. Coil rope and position it under holder. Tack top of holder down, securing rope coil in place.
- "Frame" with red grosgrain ribbon by gluing or stapling around outside edge, turning under the raw edge at end.
- Pop Babar and his family into the basket!

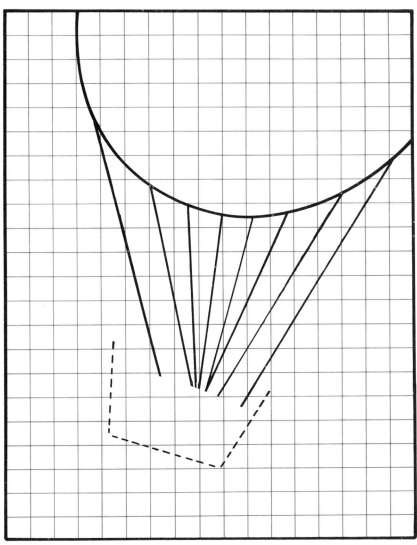

1 square = 1 inch

BACK-TO-SCHOOL SWEATER ⎯⎯⎯⎯⎯⎯⎯⎯

This turtleneck sweater is a simple classic design from Peter Pan (*see* Suppliers). You can work Babar elephants in duplicate stitch all around the bottom, just like the Peter Rabbit sweater on page 17. Boys and girls will be all ready to go back to nursery school, wearing their satchels on their backs.

MATERIALS

Peter Pan Darling double-knit yarn
Nos. 10 and 8 knitting needles
Stitch holders

To fit chest sizes: 20 (22, 24) inches
Length from back neck: 11 (12½, 14) inches
Sleeve seam: 6½ (8½, 10½) inches

Gauge: 12 sts and 16 rows = 2″ on no. 8 needles

ORDER OF WORKING

Back

Using no. 10 needles, cast on 65 (71, 77) sts.
- Ribbing row 1: (right side) K1, *p1, k1, repeat from * to end.
- Ribbing row 2: P1, *k1, p1, repeat from * to end.
- Change to no. 8 needles.
- Body row 1: Knit.
- Body row 2: Purl (stockinette stitch).
- Continue in stockinette stitch until the work measures 6¾ (7½, 8½) inches from the beginning, ending on a purl row.

Shape Armholes

- K2 together at each end of the needle on the next and every following alternate row until 23 (25, 27) sts remain, finishing on P row.
- Slip these sts onto a stitch holder. Break off yarn.

Front

- Work exactly as instructions given for back until 33 (37, 39) sts remain, finishing on a right-side row.

Shape Neck

- P22 (25, 26) sts, slip the last 11 (13, 13) sts just worked onto a stitch holder, purl to end.
- Continue to decrease at armhole edge as before on every alternate row. At the same time, K2 together at neck edge on the next 4 (4, 5) rows.
- Continue to decrease at armhole edge only until 2 sts remain. K2 together. Fasten off.
- Rejoin the yarn at neck edge to remaining sts. Work to correspond with other side, reversing all shapings.

Sleeves

- Using no. 10 needles, cast on 35 (37, 39) sts.
- Work 2 inches in rib as given for back.
- Change to no. 8 needles and stockinette stitch (1 row k, 1 row p). Continue in stockinette stitch, increasing 1 st at each end of the needle on the third and every following eighth row until 43 (47, 53) sts are on the needle.
- Continue without further increases until sleeve measures 6½ (8½, 10½) inches from beginning, finishing on a purl row.

Shape Top

- Cast off 4 sts at beginning of the next 2 rows.
- Next row: Knit.
- Next row: Purl.
- Next row: K2 together, knit to the last 2 sts, K2 together.
- Next row: Purl.
- Repeat the last 4 rows twice more, then the last 2 rows only until 7 (7, 9) sts remain, finishing on a purl row. Slip these sts onto a safety pin. Break off yarn.
- Pin the sleeves into position leaving the left back raglan open; sew in by backstitching.

Neckband

- With right side of the work facing, use no.

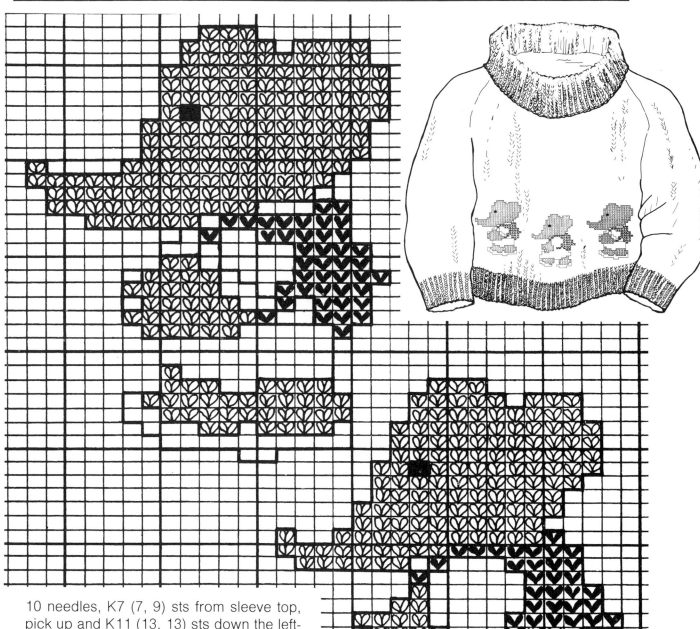

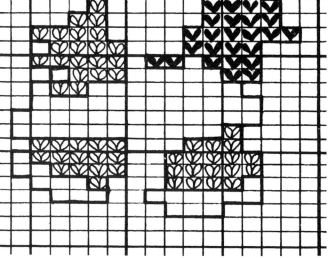

10 needles, K7 (7, 9) sts from sleeve top, pick up and K11 (13, 13) sts down the left-side neck, K11 (13, 13) sts from center front, pick up and K10 (12, 12) sts up the right-side neck, K7 (7, 9) sts from sleeve top and 23 (25, 27) sts from the back neck (69 (77, 83) sts.)

- Commencing on a second row, work in rib as given for the back, working 4½ (4½, 5) inches. Cast off in rib. Join the left back raglan, side, and sleeve seams by back-stitching, omitting rib. Join the rib by top sewing. Join the collar by top sewing reverse seam for turnback.

BABAR APPLIQUÉ BATHROBE

(Color Plates 20 and 21)

Like the sweat shirt on page 82, Babar can be stitched on fleecy fabric, such as a terry robe, using the Trace Erase™ fabric method. Alternatively, stitch Babar like Kermit on page 49 as a patch that you can cut out and appliqué.

MATERIALS

Purchased robe or clothing article of your choice
Black cotton floss
Crewel wools
Trace Erase™ material

ORDER OF WORKING

- Trace the full-size patterns here and on page 80 on Trace Erase™ fabric with a fine-point permanent marker.
- Baste Trace Erase™ fabric in position on the robe.
- Stitch each character, using simple long satin stitches to fill each area (refer to Color Plate 21).
- Outline each character in stem stitch with three threads of black cotton floss and add French-knot eyes.
- Tear away Trace Erase™ fabric when stitching is complete. Remove any bits and pieces by rubbing with the flat points of a pair of scissors.

Plate 20. "BABAR" appliqué bathrobe (page 79). Project based on the Babar series of books by Laurent de Brunhoff and published by Random House, Inc. Reproduced with permission.

Plate 21.   Detail of "BABAR" bathrobe (Plate 20).

Plate 22. "WINNIE THE POOH" needlepoint canvas (page 94). Based on an illustration from *The House at Pooh Corner* by A. A. Milne. Copyright 1928 by E. P. Dutton & Co., Inc. Copyright renewed 1956 by A. A. Milne. Reprinted by permission of the publisher, E. P. Dutton.

Plate 23. "POOH AND THE RABBIT HOLE" cross-stitch picture (pages 88–89).

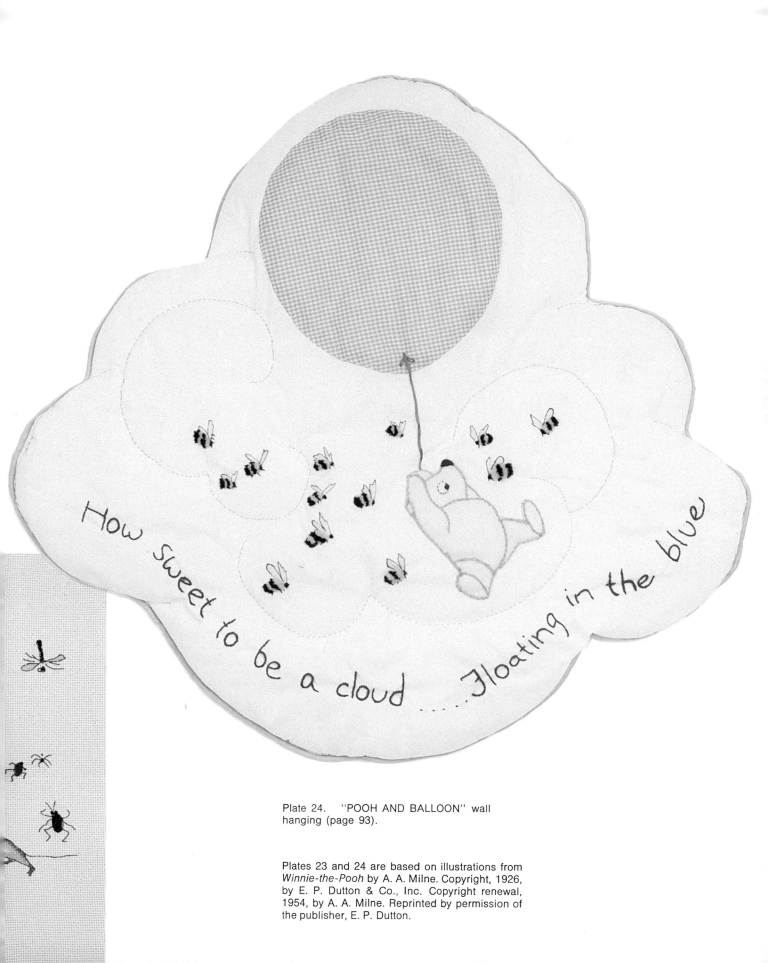

Plate 24. "POOH AND BALLOON" wall hanging (page 93).

There is nothing—

absolutely nothing—

half so much worth doing—

as simply messing

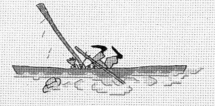

about in boats

25.

26.

27.

...Simply messing about in boats...

From *Winnie-the-Pooh,* by A. A. Milne. Copyright 1926 E. P. Dutton & Co., Inc. Copyright renewed 1954 by A. A. Milne. Reprinted by permission of the publisher, E. P. Dutton.

WINNIE THE POOH AND THE WIND IN THE WILLOWS

Plate 25 *(opposite).* "WIND IN THE WILLOWS" boating panel (page 83).

Plate 26 *(opposite).* "SIMPLY MESSING ABOUT IN BOATS" sweatshirt (page 82).

Plate 27 *(opposite).* Detail of sweatshirt (Plate 26).

From *The Wind in the Willows,* by Kenneth Grahame. Copyright 1933, 1953 Charles Scribner's Sons. Renewal copyright © 1961 Ernest H. Shepard. Reprinted with permission.

"Born in 1882, small of course, but slowly grew." The son of a London schoolmaster, Alan Alexander Milne could read when he was two, and at the age of eleven he won a scholarship to Westminster School. From the very beginning he wrote verses and humorous stories and later became a successful playwright. But the publication of his first book, *When We Were Very Young,* in 1924 proved to be a momentous event in Milne's career. It seemed simple at the time. Since he spent so much time writing at home, it was natural for the father to find inspiration from his son and write stories about him. If the Winnie the Pooh stories are wonderful, an integral part of them is the inimitable illustrations by Ernest H. Shepard. Through them, Christopher Robin's friends, Pooh Bear and Piglet and Eeyore, really come alive. And, of course, as Christopher Robin would have said, "How can you leave out Kanga and Roo and Tigger and Owl and Rabbit?" Their economy of line makes them perfect for needlework of all kinds. In fact, a whole book could be taken up with ideas from these illustrations alone.

Another favorite, also illustrated by Ernest H. Shepard, is *The Wind in the Willows,* by Kenneth Grahame. It is the story of a water rat and a toad and many friends, who interact freely with the human beings around them. In 1933, when he was first asked to make black-and-white drawings for the story, Shepard visited Grahame at his home. There he walked along the riverbank, making sketches for the setting and seeing where the houses of the little animals might be. "I love these little people," Grahame said. "Be kind to them." And later: "I'm glad you made them real." From the past history of all these books, it is certain that they will go on being real for people of all ages for many years to come—just as your needlework inspired by them will continue to be enjoyed by everyone, regardless of age.

"SIMPLY MESSING ABOUT IN BOATS SWEATSHIRT"

(Color Plates 26 and 27)

Stitching a design on a stretchy fabric such as a sweatshirt is easy, thanks to Trace Erase™ fabric. You stitch through both layers and tear away the excess Trace Erase™ fabric from around the design, leaving no sign of how the design was transferred.

MATERIALS

Sweatshirt
Cotton floss
Trace Erase™ fabric

ORDER OF WORKING

- Trace the outline of the pattern on pages 84–85 on Trace Erase™ fabric with a fine-point permanent marker (see page 132).
- Separate the 6-strand floss and use 2 strands for outlines and 3 strands for everything else.
- Work the design as follows (the angle of the satin stitch and long and short stitch is shown by dotted lines on the diagram): grasses, boat, and Badger's clothes in satin stitch; animals in long and short shading; oars in split stitch; fishing basket in burden stitch; and all outlines and lettering in stem stitch.
- When stitching is completed, tear away Trace Erase™ fabric.

The sweatshirt and boating panel on these pages are based on drawings by Ernest H. Shepard in *The Wind in the Willows,* by Kenneth Grahame, copyright 1933, 1953 Charles Scribner's Sons, renewal copyright © 1961 Ernest H. Shepard. Reprinted with permission.

WIND IN THE WILLOWS BOATING PANEL

(Color Plate 25)

The perfect gift for boating enthusiasts, this panel may be cross stitched easily with the method described on page 134. Finished panel is 13″ wide by 22″ long.

MATERIALS

17 × 26″ Cream #14 Aida cloth
Cotton floss
Trace Erase™ fabric

ORDER OF WORKING

- Establish the vertical and horizontal center of panel.
- Baste guidelines.
- Trace pattern outlines on Trace Erase™ fabric with a fine-point permanent marker.
- Referring to the photo, arrange traced pictures on cloth, allowing space for lettering.
- Baste in position.
- Separate 6-strand floss to use 3 strands for cross stitches and 1 strand for backstitch outlines.
- Work each line of lettering from the center out, referring to the graphed charts on pages 86–87 and the photo.
- Backstitch all outlines in black, but use blue for water. Work right through Trace Erase™ and cloth.
- Tear away the Trace Erase™ fabric.
- Referring to Color Plate 25, fill in each area with cross stitch using 3 strands of floss.

. . . Simply messing

about in boats . . .

There is nothing —

absolutely nothing —

half so much worth doing —

half so much worth doing —

as simply messing

about in boats

87

POOH AND THE RABBIT HOLE CROSS-STITCH _

(Color Plate 23)

The story of Pooh, who had eaten far too much honey and gotten stuck in Rabbit's hole, is one of the favorites of all the charming stories about the indomitable bear. Working in cross stitch normally has a disadvantage, since the square grid necessitates angular shapes. The integrity of the drawing is maintained here by the unique method of first outlining the drawing on fabric, then filling it in like a coloring book with cross stitch (see page 134). The finished

picture is 14 × 36″ overall, with 9 × 28″ embroidery.

MATERIALS

7 yards Cream # 14 Aida cloth
Cotton floss
9 × 28″ Trace Erase™ fabric

ORDER OF WORKING

• Outline the pattern on pages 90–91 on

88

Trace Erase™ fabric with a fine-point permanent marker.

- Baste in position on Aida cloth.
- Separate 6-strand floss and use 1 strand to work all outlines in backstitch. Work all outlines in black except twigs and grasses, in green and tan, stitching through Trace Erase™ fabric and Aida cloth.
- Tear away Trace Erase™ fabric inside and outside the design. You now have a "coloring book" outline to fill in with cross stitch!

- Referring to Color Plate 23 as a guide, fill in each area with cross stitch, using 3 strands of floss. Compensate to fill the corners with half-stitches as required. Finishing touches may be clipped turkey-work tails on the rabbits.

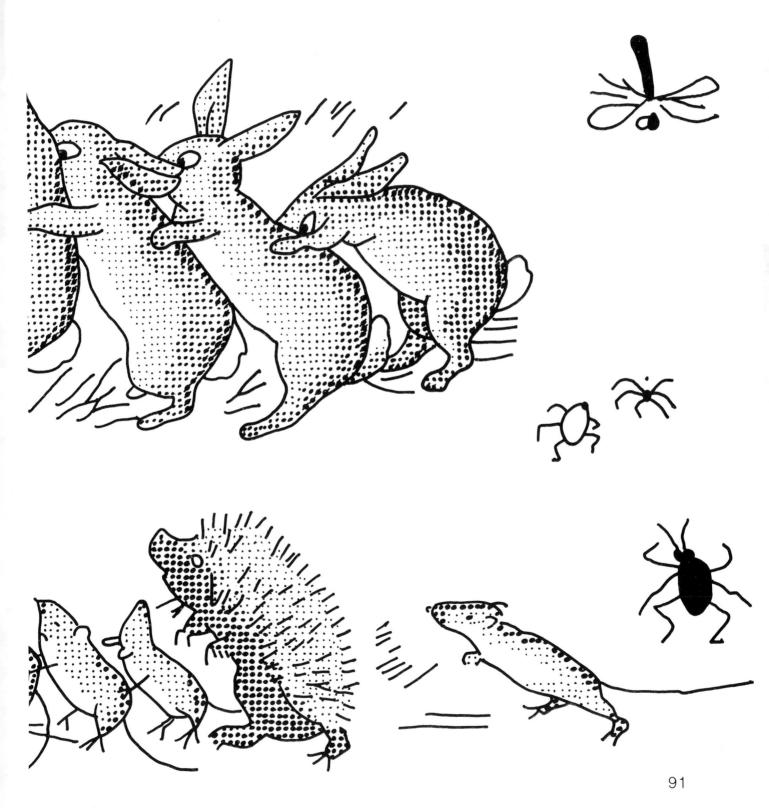

How Sweet to be a cloud ..... floating in the blue

POOH AND BALLOON WALL HANGING

(Color Plate 24)

Pooh floating like a cloud in the sky could make a charming wall hanging or center of a quilt. Appliqué a blue gingham balloon and yellow felt Pooh bear, and stitch the bees realistically in turkey work. Finished hanging is approximately 26 × 24″.

MATERIALS

2 yards white fabric
10 × 12″ blue gingham
5 × 6″ pale gold felt
Crewel wool
Cotton floss
2½ yards blue piping
"Extra loft" quilt batting

ORDER OF WORKING

- Enlarge pattern and trace onto white fabric with Trace Erase™ pen.
- Trace and cut the balloon out of gingham, allowing ⅜″ all around for turnbacks. Clip the turnbacks so they will lie flat. Cut the batting to fit under the balloon. Layer the batting, then the balloon, and baste in position on white fabric. Sew down with small stitches.
- Trace and cut the actual size Pooh without turnbacks. Cut batting to layer under Pooh, and appliqué as for balloon.
- Embroider features with floss and work a stem-stitch outline with crewel wool through all layers.
- To complete the embroidery: Bee wings, floss straight stitches; bodies, clipped turkey work with crewel wool; balloon string, long and short stitch, anchored to balloon with two lazy daisy stitches; lettering, stem stitch with cotton floss.
- Cut out the cloud front and cut the backing from the remaining white fabric, being certain to allow ½″ all around for the seam allowance. Cut batting to layer between front and back.
- Baste batting securely behind cloud front.
- Lay backing face down on the front and

1 square = 1 inch

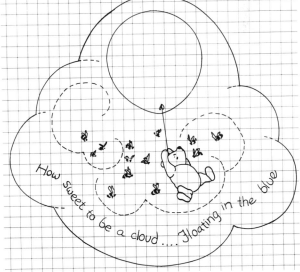

baste, enclosing blue piping to the inside of the seam at the same time. Stitch around, leaving the opening to turn. Clip the curves, turn, and stitch the opening closed.

- Use blue floss to quilt puffy swirls into the cloud through all layers. Remove basting.

CHRISTOPHER ROBIN AND POOH NEEDLEPOINT

(Color Plate 22)

Christopher Robin and Pooh can also be done in cross stitch using the method described on page 89 for the rabbit hole picture.

MATERIALS

#14 Mono canvas
Persian wools

ORDER OF WORKING

- Trace the design on page 95 on paper with a black permanent marker. Lay it on a table or firm surface and hold it in position with masking tape.

- Trace the design on canvas, using a Trace Erase™ pen or fine-point permanent marker.

- Draw the design with a fine light line (a heavy black line may be hard to cover with light-colored wools). Draw the design as you would on paper, ignoring the mesh of the canvas, and make the lines smooth and flowing. You will find that you can better interpret curves with your needle if you draw them smoothly on the canvas, instead of anticipating the stitches with a zigzag drawing that follows the canvas. If you want to paint your design in color, use waterproof marking pens and refer to Color Plate 22 for suggested colors.

KATE GREENAWAY

"People laugh at me, I am so delighted and pleased with things, and say I see with rose-colored spectacles. What do you think—is it not a beautiful world?"

Born in 1846, Kate Greenaway spent her entire life drawing and painting children. Through her drawings she created a whole world of her own idealized version of children, in costumes of an earlier age. Working from live models, she nevertheless invested each painting with her own special imaginative style.

The original sketch shown here, from the author's collection, has never been published before. This is unique because Greenaway was a most prolific artist who had hundreds of her sketches reproduced all over the world.

THE SUNBONNET BABIES

Eulalie Osgood Grover, the author of *The Sunbonnet Babies Book,* wrote the charming little primer to teach children to read. The simplicity of the text and drawings by Bertha Corbett Melcher have made it a classic that has been emulated in hundreds of different ways ever since.

The needlework ideas from both these books will hopefully start you thinking and give you inspiration. As well as following the designs shown here, you can use the outlined cross-stitch technique shown for Pooh on page 89 to adapt any of the illustrations for your own use, even the sketches on this page.

Plate 28. "SUNBON-NET GIRLS" crib cover and crib bumpers (page 108).

Plate 29. "KATE GREEN-AWAY" dolls (page 118).

30.

31.

32.

Plate 30. "KATE GREEN-AWAY" boy's suit (page 116).

Plate 31. Detail of boy's suit (Plate 30).

Plate 32. "KATE GREEN-AWAY" wedding pillow (page 126).

Plate 33. "SUNBONNET GIRLS" dress (page 116).

Plate 34. Detail of dress (Plate 33).

Plate 35. "SUNBONNET GIRLS" flower garden panel (page 112).

May day improve on day

May joy and friendship

and year on year

crown your days

34.

33.

5.

36.

Plate 36. "WATER BABIES" cross-stitch quilt and pillows (page 97).

Plate 37. "ROSE FLOWER FAIRY" panel (page 104).

Plate 38. "JASMINE FLOWER FAIRY" panel (page 104).

37.

38.

THE WATER BABIES

The moving story of little Tom, the chimney sweep, who ran into the river but instead of drowning was magically turned into a water baby, was written by Charles Kingsley in 1851. The original illustrations, by Jessie Willcox Smith, are some of the most beautiful of her exquisite work.

Jessie Willcox Smith painted children all her life and has left us a legacy of beautiful work. The obituary poem written at the death of Kate Greenaway could equally be applied to her:

> Farewell; kind heart And if there be
> In that unshared immensity,
> Child—Angels, they will welcome thee.
> Clean-souled, clear-eyed, unspoiled, discreet,
> Thou gav'st thy gifts to make life sweet;
> There shall be flowers about thy feet.

The cross-stitch quilt of this design (page 99) can be done on prequilted fabric, by counting the design out on specially printed Trace Erase™ fabric. Alternatively, you can make stencils of the designs and paint them on fabric, like the quilt on page 9.

THE FLOWER FAIRIES

To English author Cecily Mary Barker every flower has its own flower child. In a series of charming little books, she combined the verses and paintings of each of her favorites. On the next pages you will find the Rose and Jasmine Flower Fairies, with backgrounds painted in soft watercolors on the cloth so that they closely resemble the paintings that inspired them.

The designs are worked in crewel wools, combined with the sheen of cotton floss, and the finished picture can be mounted in a soft fabric frame. (Instructions for making fabric frames are on page 105.) The Flower Fairies could also be interpreted in cross stitch, using the method described on page 134.

WATER BABIES CROSS-STITCH QUILT AND PILLOWS

(Color Plate 36)

Jessie Willcox Smith's charming drawings of the Water Babies are perfect for cross stitch to be used on quilts, pillows, or as a bathroom set with matching shower curtain, latch-hook bath mat, and lid cover. The finished quilt is 44 × 58″, the pillow 15″ square.

MATERIALS

Cotton floss
Quilt batting
Fiberfill

3¼ yards white fabric 45″ wide for the quilt
1 yard white fabric 45″ wide for each pillow
Bias binding and piping to edge the quilt and pillows
Quilting thread
Waste canvas (5 mesh; or 10 mesh working each cross stitch over 2 threads)

ORDER OF WORKING

- Refer to the charts and the photo, on pages 98–103.
- To arrange designs on the quilt top or pil-

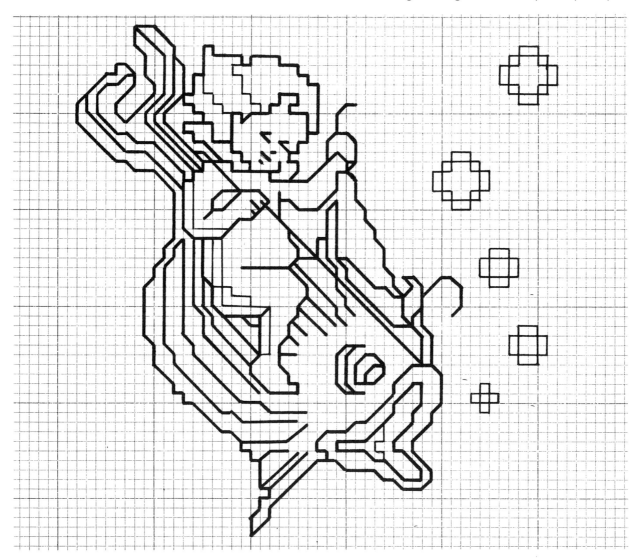

Finished size fits a 10 × 12" rectangle

Finished size fits a 6 × 10½" rectangle

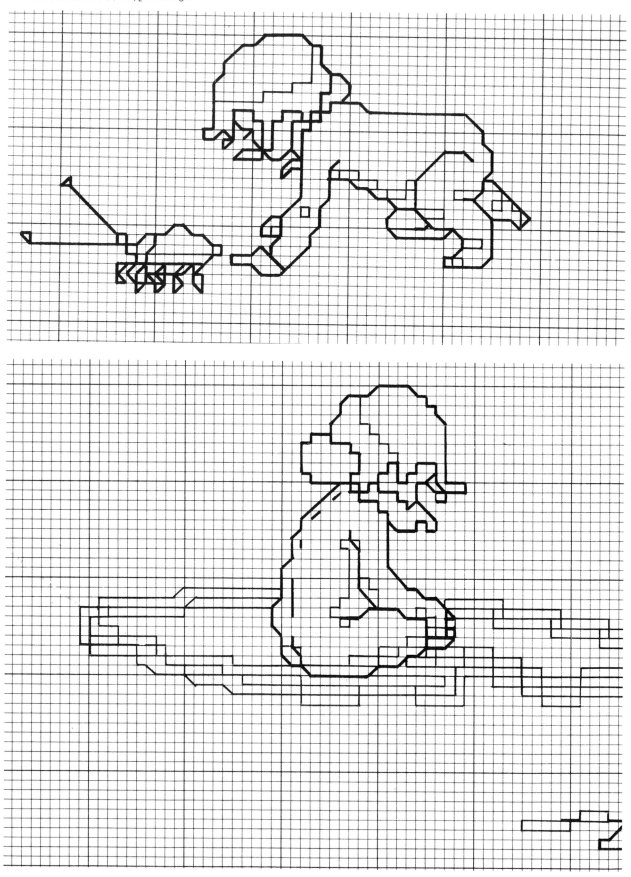

100

low top, cut tissue paper rectangles the finished size indicated on each graph and mark their position with basting threads.

- Cut waste canvas the size of tissue paper rectangles plus 1″ all around. (Waste canvas, a thin open-weave scrim available by the yard, is used for transferring geometric designs in cross stitch onto any fabric that does not have a clearly defined weave, such as muslin or cotton broadcloth.) Baste the canvas over the areas where the patterns are to be.

- Stretch the whole thing in an embroidery frame, and stitch the pattern through both thicknesses, keeping your stitches even by counting the threads of the canvas.

- When the design is finished, unravel the threads of the canvas at the edges and draw them out, one by one. If your fabric is washable, it may be easier to do this if you soak the embroidery in cold water, which softens the sizing in the canvas and loosens the threads enough to allow them to slip out easily.

- Alternately, use Trace Erase™ fabric printed with a grid, which would replace the waste canvas. Baste the grid-printed fabric on top, and when the work is complete just dissolve it in water.

- Use a Trace Erase™ pen to mark the quilting pattern, such as waves and bubbles, as shown in the photo on page 98 and in Color Plate 36. Baste the embroidered top, batting, and lining together with a running stitch and quilting thread. Quilt over the pattern you have drawn.

- Finish the edges of the quilt with bias seam binding and assemble the pillows with piped edges.

Finished size fits a 10½ × 19″ rectangle

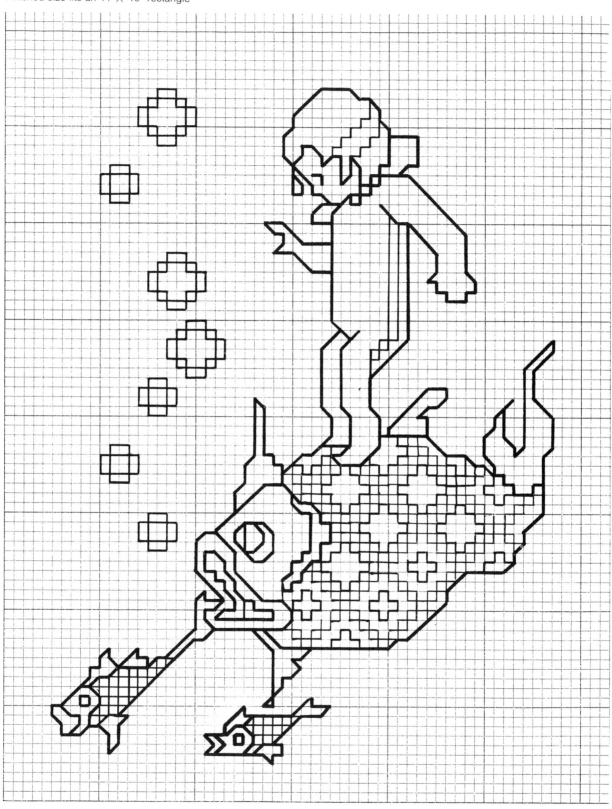

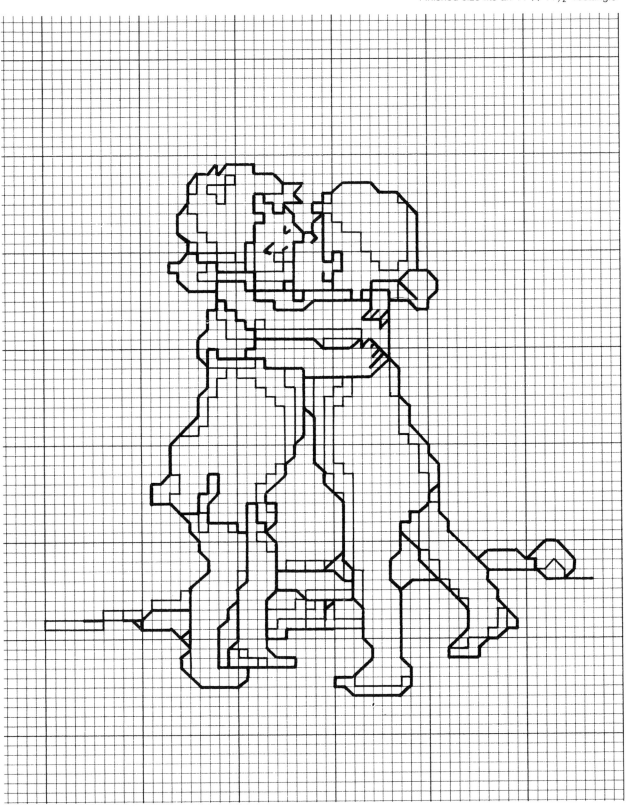

FLOWER FAIRIES

(Color Plates 37 and 38)

The two Flower Fairies, Rose and Jasmine, may be worked in a combination of painting and stitching as described below. Alternatively, work them with the cross stitch method on page 134 or in the painted and quilted technique on page 9.

MATERIALS

½ yard cotton broadcloth or white linen
Acrylic paints
Crewel wool
Cotton floss

ORDER OF WORKING

- Outline the full size design on pages 106–107 on fabric.
- Paint the background with the water-color effect using acrylics (*see* Color Plates 38 and 39).
- Paint the body, face, arms and legs with flat color in flesh tones.
- Outline the painted shapes that will be left open with backstitch.

- Work flowers, leaves, and fairies' wings in long and short stitch using 1 strand of yarn.
- To give added sheen to the wings and jasmine flowers, overlay the wool with long and short stitches in 3 strands of cotton floss.
- Work fairies' hair in rows of stem stitch.
- Work clothing in lines of split stitch, following the contours of the drawing. Work highlights with white floss stitched on top afterwards.
- If desired, highlight features with 1 strand of floss.

PADDED FRAMES FOR FLOWER FAIRIES ___

Padded frames, ready for covering, are available in craft shops, but to make your own, in the exact size you require, follow these simple steps.

MATERIALS

1½" wide stretcher strips of desired length
Fabric 8" longer and wider than desired frame size
Batting
Foam rubber
All-purpose white glue
Staple gun

ORDER OF WORKING

- Assemble stretcher strips.
- Cut foam rubber to fit exactly on top of stretcher strip frame and glue lightly in place (Diagram 1).
- Lay narrow strips of batting in place on top to raise and pad the center of each bar. Cut a square piece of fabric 4" larger in both length and width than outside measurements of stretcher strips.
- At each inner corner of the frame, lightly glue a strip of fabric in place for corner camouflage.
- Place and pin fabric on top of padded frame.
- Beginning from the center, cut four slits in the fabric, cutting out to each corner (Diagram 2). Next, fold and stretch fabric around to the back and staple or tack in place (Diagram 3). Do not pull too tightly at the corners.
- Fold outer edges of fabric around frame and staple in place, folding and pleating fullness at corners. Trim away excess fabric.

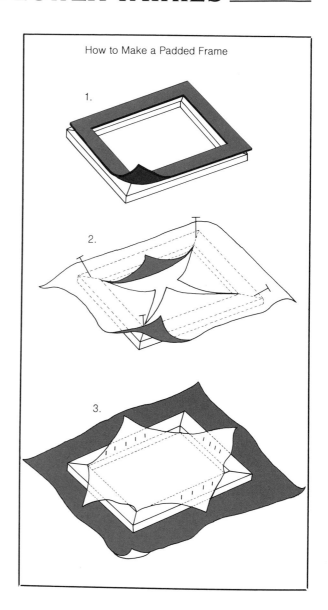

How to Make a Padded Frame

1.

2.

3.

SUNBONNET CRIB COVER AND BUMPERS

(Color Plate 28)

You can either paint or appliqué the Sunbonnet girls. The simplicity of the design with its focus on colorful fabrics makes it ideal for either method.

MATERIALS

3⅜ yards white cotton 45" wide (1 yard for quilt top, 2⅜ yards for bumpers)
1 yard calico cotton 45" wide for lining
Contrasting calico cotton for binding
Assorted cotton prints for appliqué
Acrylic paints
Paint brush
Cotton floss
Quilt batting
1" thick foam (25½ × 48" or six 8 × 25½" pieces)
Vogue Pattern 2535 for crib bumpers

ORDER OF WORKING

- Establish the center of the quilt (size 34 × 44" plus ½" turnbacks) by folding the fabric in half and half again.
- Trace the full-size patterns on pages 110–111 in the center, using Trace Erase™ marker.
- Trace separate pattern pieces on Trace Erase™ fabric.
- Pin and baste on top of the fabrics for appliqué. Make sure the grain of the fabric on the appliqué runs parallel with that of the base material.
- To apply fabrics by machine, do not cut out each shape. Pin and baste rectangles of Trace Erase™ fabric in position on the design and run around the outlines with a machine overlock stitch. Afterward, tear away the Trace Erase™ fabric close to stitching around edges.
- To apply by hand, pin and baste Trace Erase™ fabric on top of each fabric for appliqué. Machine stitch or work a hand running stitch around all outlines.
- Tear away Trace Erase™. Trim the shapes,

leaving ¼" turnbacks, all around. Snip and notch the turnbacks and finger-press them back to make smooth curves. Where one fabric will overlap another, do not turn back, but leave edges flat.

- Pin in position on the fabric and sew down with tiny invisible stitches at right angles to the edge. For smaller pieces where taking turnbacks would be impractical, pin them flat on the fabric and turn back each piece with your needle as you sew it down.
- Outline with stem stitch with 4 strands of cotton floss, and add embroidery details, such as arms, basket of flowers, French knots, etc.
- The "powdering" of small flowers over the background can be stitched with padded satin stitch and French knots or appliquéd as described above. On the quilt and matching bumpers in Color Plate 28 the flowers were painted. For this, follow the instructions on page 16.
- Baste the quilt top, batting, and lining together. With either a long machine stitch or even running stitches and quilting thread, quilt around the appliquéd motif.
- Use 6-strand floss to quilt the two border rectangles with a chain stitch. Bind the outside edges of the quilt with contrasting calico.

110

SUNBONNET FLOWER GARDEN

Each flower in this garden has its own textured stitch worked quite simply without shading. First establish your color scheme by choosing the fabric for appliquéing the sunbonnet girl in the center, then use up leftover yarns to make the garden a collage of color. Buttonhole stitch, French knots, satin stitch, and bullion knots can be crowded close, just like a real garden in groups of flowers, making a background for the sunbonnet girl in appliqué.

MATERIALS

Off-white linen or other suitable fabric
Cotton floss
Perle cotton
Small pieces of pink and yellow felt and 2 different calico prints
3½″ of narrow pregathered lace

ORDER OF WORKING

- Trace design to fabric with a Trace Erase™ pen.
- Separate the floss and use 2 strands to begin your embroidery, but by all means experiment with 3 or 4 strands where you might like more texture. Use perle cotton undivided.
- For flowers try lazy daisy stitch, French knots, bullion knots, and buttonhole stitch.
- For leaves, grasses, and stems, experiment with straight, stem, satin, or fishbone stitches. Lazy daisies make great leaves as well. Scatter a few seeding stitches in the background. Be sure to work the Sunbonnet gardener's shoes in satin stitch.
- Stitch pregathered lace to embroidered panel or position for bottom of dress appliqúe.
- Trace and appliqué shapes to appliqué bonnet and dress in two different calico prints, making sure to add turnbacks. Snip the turnbacks along edges so they will lay flat. Hem the turnback at the lower edge of

the dress so it can be left free to reveal the "petticoat" of pregathered lace. Baste the shapes in place and sew down with tiny stitches at right angles to the edge.

- Cut the arm and basket piece from felt and stitch it in place.
- Embellish appliqué with stem stitch outlines, buttonhole rows for the weave of the basket, and additional flowers in both hand and basket.

SUNBONNET GIRL'S DRESS

(Color Plates 33 and 34)

The sunbonnet girls in their garden of flowers can be embroidered in cotton floss on any little girl's frock. To make a dress exactly like the one shown here, see "Almost Ready to Wear" under Suppliers on page 158.

MATERIALS

Purchased infant's dress or completed kit
Cotton floss

ORDER OF WORKING

- Trace the full-size design onto the finished dress with Trace Erase™ pen or a hard, sharp pencil.
- Separate 6-strand floss and use 1 strand to work long and short filling stitches and 2 strands for everything else.
- Referring to Color Plates 33 and 34 for color suggestions, work the outlines and flower stems in stem stitch, the grass with straight stitches.
- Make baskets by filling them with long vertical stitches evenly spaced. Then, with a blunt needle, weave over and under the stitches to achieve the effect shown. Use long and short stitches and tiny seeding stitches to fill the areas of clothing.
- Make bullion-knot flowers with lazy daisy leaves. Complete the dress by working five additional flowers scattered along both sides of the hem, as shown in the photo opposite.

KATE GREENAWAY BOY'S SUIT

(Color Plates 30 and 31)

This charming Kate Greenaway figure for a boy could be embroidered on an outfit like the one shown here or on your little fisherman's tee shirt! To make an outfit exactly like the one shown here, see "Almost Ready to Wear" under Suppliers on page 158.

MATERIALS

Purchased infant's suit or completed kit
Cotton floss

ORDER OF WORKING

- Trace the full-size design onto the finished suit with a Trace Erase™ pen or a hard, sharp pencil.
- Separate 6-strand floss and use 1 strand for working long and short stitch and 2 strands for everything else.
- Referring to Color Plates 30 and 31, work outlines in stem stitch and grasses and stems with straight stitches. Make French knots for flowers and a single lazy daisy for each cattail. Use long and short stitch as your filling stitch. Add finishing details to face and clothing with tiny seed stitches and French knots. The birds are simple fly stitches. Work additional cattails between tucks at either side of the bib, as shown in the photo opposite.

116

KATE GREENAWAY DOLLS

These Kate Greenaway dolls are based on the idea of a floppy Raggedy Ann doll—very simple to make and lifelike to play with. Their clothes can be as exotic or as simple as you wish, depending on whether you add embroidery touches and use velvets, silks, and so on.

MATERIALS

½ yard ecru cotton
½ yard white cotton
Small pieces red-and-white striped cotton
Blue velvet
Gold felt
⅓ yard pink floral print
½ yard matching light pink fabric
Small piece matching dark pink fabric
Small skein light yellow craft yarn
Small skein brown craft yarn
Cotton floss
3 yards rust ribbon ⅝" wide
1 yard very narrow blue ribbon ⅛" wide
Small pieces of ribbon to make flowers
Fiberfill
3 white buttons
9" piece ¼" elastic

ORDER OF WORKING

Note that no seam allowances have been added to pattern pieces on pages 121–125.

- Using a Trace Erase™ pen on ecru cotton, trace hands and heads, front and back, for both dolls, and for the girl's body only, sleeves and legs. Trace the boy's legs on red-and-white striped fabric and the boy's body and sleeves on white fabric. Separate 6-strand floss and use 2 strands to embroider features with satin and stem stitch. Cut out traced pieces, making certain to allow for turnings.
- Fold each leg piece right sides together and seam the open edge and bottom. Turn and stuff a small amount of fiberfill in the bottom to make "feet." Stitch across the leg to keep the foot stuffing in place.
- With right sides facing, seam short ends of body together. Placing this seam at center back, baste bottom of body closed in a flat seam that encloses the tops of the legs as well. Stitch and turn to right side.
- Sew the head front and back together, right sides facing, leaving the bottom of the neck open. Turn. Stuff firmly.
- Stuff the body firmly. With running stitches, draw the top edge closed around the base of the doll's neck. Stitch securely.
- Stitch pieces of each hand with right sides together, leaving straight top edge open. Turn, stuff, and slip stitch closed.
- Narrowly hem end of sleeves. Fold with right sides facing and seam the long edges together. Turn. With running stitches gather along the line indicated and draw stitches up to form sleeve ruffles secured with small stitches to top edge of hands.
- Fold raw edge at top of sleeves to the wrong side in the narrow hem secured with running stitches. Gather top edges together as you do so and then stitch sleeve top to doll's shoulders with tiny stitches.
- Cut shoes for each doll from deep pink fabric. Narrowly hem straight top edges of shoe pieces. Seam right sides together, leaving hemmed edges open. Turn. Slip over the end of foot and stitch in place with running stitches about ¼" from top edge, gathering slightly as you do so. Tie a 9" length of ⅛" wide blue ribbon securely over stitches.

FINISHING BOY

- From white cotton, cut out a strip of bias 3 × 14" for neck ruffle. Seam short ends. Then, fold in half lengthwise and sew edges together with running stitch that you draw up to form ruffle after slipping it over doll's head. Gather and stitch raw edges to doll's body from the underside of ruffle.

- Sew long loops of brown yarn to the back of the head and a shorter loop along the front top and sides to form hair.
- Cut gold felt hat piece. Carefully cut center out for top of hat and use remaining "doughnut" for brim. Cut a strip from the same felt 1½" wide × 12" long. With tiny stitches close to edge, sew short ends of strip together. Then sew one edge of ring thus formed to edge of hat top, and sew remaining edge to inside edge of brim. On the outside, tack a ribbon hat band in place and tack hat on to doll's head.
- Cut pants from blue velvet. With right sides together, stitch from front to back along the side and crotch seams. Slash top of crotch seam almost to stitching. Hem pant legs. Turn top edge ½" and stitch, enclosing 4" of elastic at the back. Adjust and stitch ends of elastic at side seams. Sew 3 buttons at top front of pants as shown in photo on page 119. Pull pants on doll.

FINISHING GIRL

- Cut a 6 × 1" bias strip for collar. Fold lengthwise and seam long edge. Turn. Slip stitch base of strip around the doll's neck to form a standup collar. Turn raw end edges in at center back and stitch together.
- Make hair like the boy's from yellow yarn.
- To make the skirt, cut a 3½" strip of pink floral fabric the width of the fabric for ruffle. Cut remaining 8½" to a 28" width. Seam 8½" ends, leaving 2" open at top of skirt. Clean-finish 2" edges. Gather top edge to fit over center 10" of 1 yard of ribbon. Stitch in place. Seam short ends of ruffle. Fold rule in half with *wrong* sides together. With running stitches, gather raw edges together, adjusting to fit around bottom edge of skirt. Sew in place from wrong side of the skirt. Tie skirt on doll.
- Cut 2 shawl pieces from pink fabric for top and lining and make ruffle as for skirt bottom from strip cut 1¼" × 45". Stitch ruffle

around outside edge of top of shawl. Press turnings under for lining and baste in place. Slip stitch around. Wrap around doll's shoulders and tuck ends into front waistband of skirt.
- Cut hat crown and brim from light pink fabric and brim lining from dark pink. Seam lining to brim, right sides together, leaving inside curve open. Clip seam allowances and turn. Hem straight edge of crown, enclosing 5" of elastic in hem. Secure elastic at each end. Gather entire curved edge of crown with a running stitch, adjusting to fit along raw edge of brim. Baste, then stitch. Slip stitch facing seam closed. Tack 1½ yards of ribbon across brim, leaving ends for ties.

Making Ribbon Roses

(see diagrams opposite)

- Roll one end of a ribbon about six turns to make a tight tube. Bend the base of the tube up slightly and sew a few stitches to hold. This forms the center of the rose. (Diagram 1.)
- To make petals, continue turning ribbon end toward you, folding ribbon down so its edge is lined up with the tube (Diagram 2).
- Roll the tube across the ribbon end to form a cone; wind folded ribbon around tube. When the tube lies parallel to the remaining ribbon, take a few stitches to hold the petal you just made (Diagram 3). Keep folding the ribbon over in the same direction.
- Continue making petals until the rose is the desired size, shaping the rose as you work and sewing each petal to the base of rose. If you wind tightly, buds are formed. Looser petals make full-blown roses; narrow ribbons form rosettes (Diagram 4).
- Finish by folding the ribbon end over so the end is on the stitched base. Sew the end to the base; trim excess ribbon to about 1". Sew the rose in the desired position.

Making Ribbon Roses

1.   2.   3.   4.

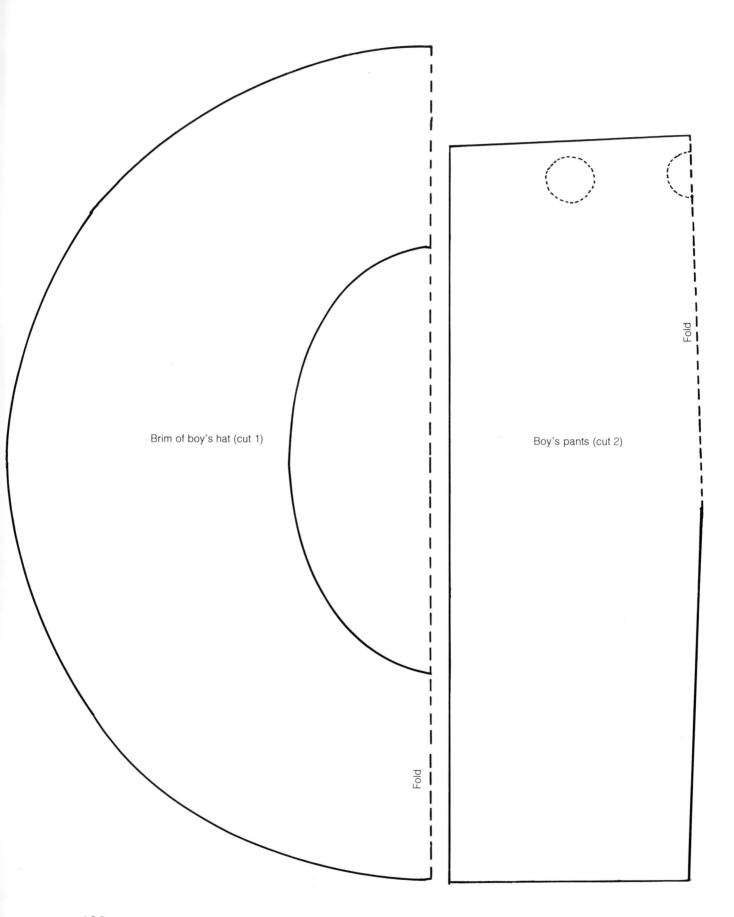

Brim of boy's hat (cut 1)

Boy's pants (cut 2)

Fold

Fold

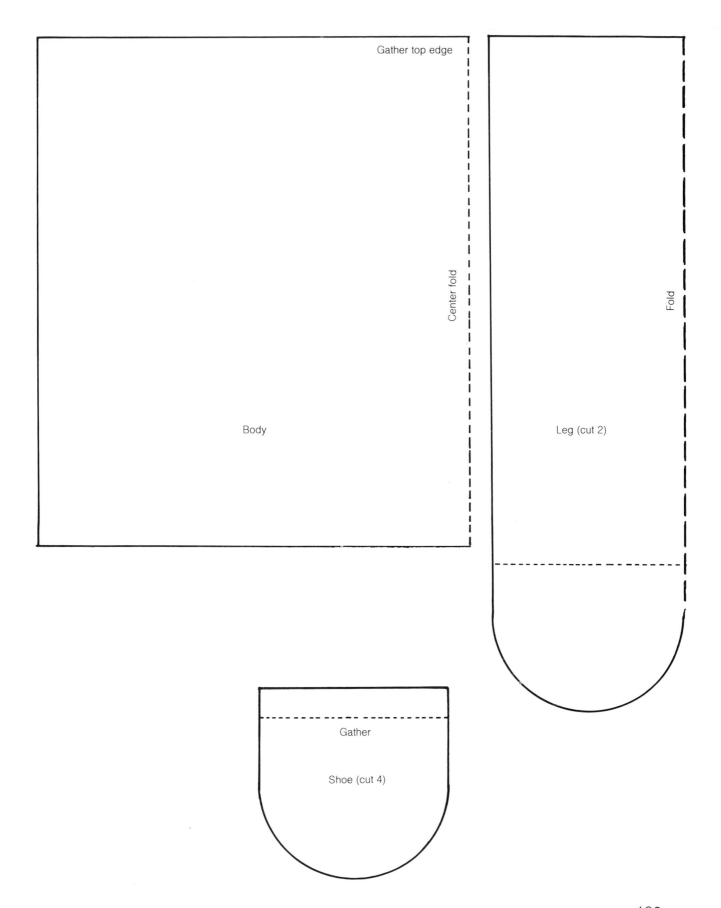

Gather top edge

Center fold

Body

Fold

Leg (cut 2)

Gather

Shoe (cut 4)

123

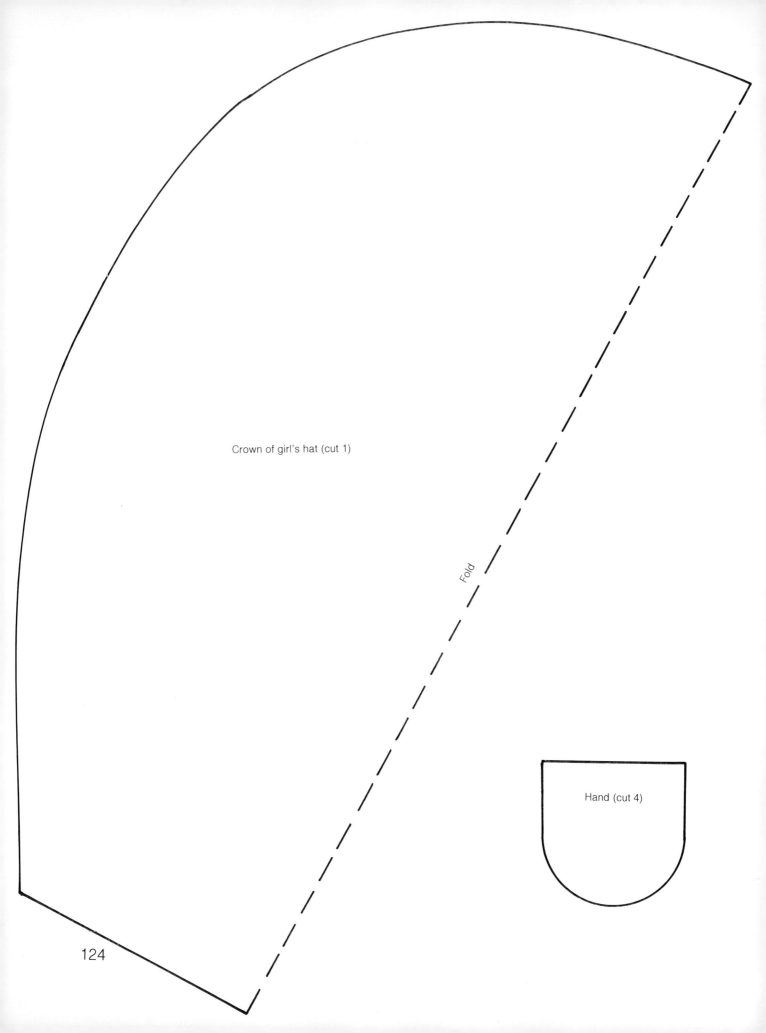

Crown of girl's hat (cut 1)

Fold

Hand (cut 4)

124

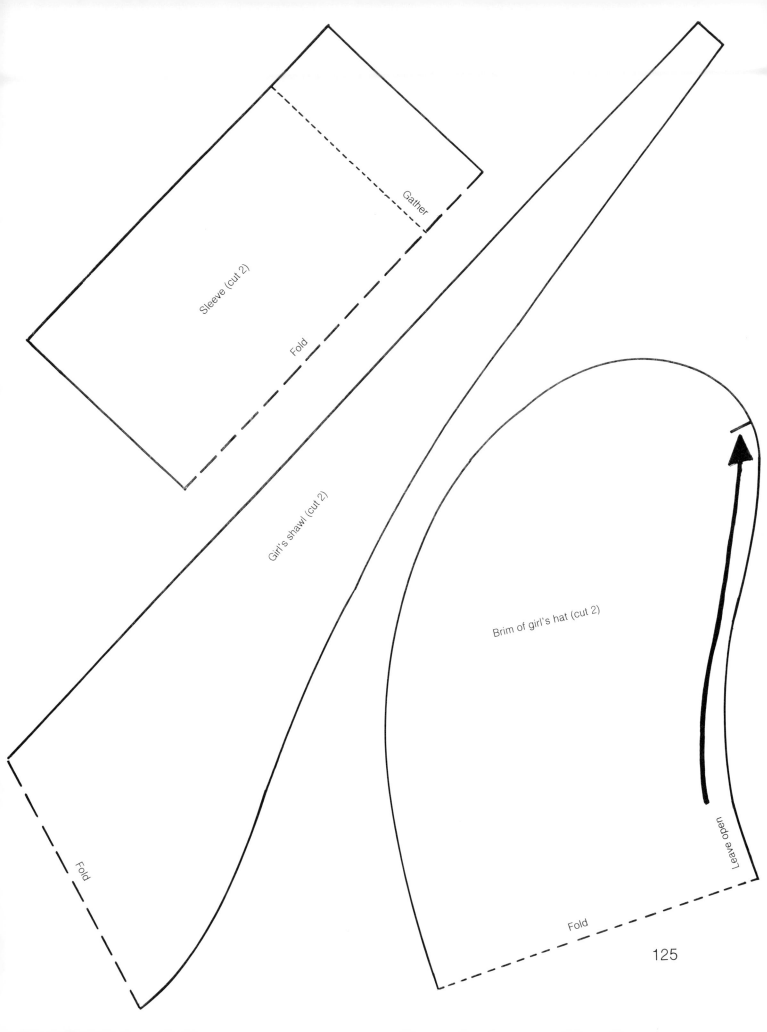

Sleeve (cut 2)

Gather

Fold

Girl's shawl (cut 2)

Brim of girl's hat (cut 2)

Fold

Leave open

Fold

125

and year on year

May joy and friendship

May you embroider every day

crown your days

KATE GREENAWAY WEDDING PILLOW_____

(Color Plate 32)

Three children bearing a crown of flowers make the centerpiece for a perfect wedding pillow present with good wishes for the young couple's future. The message can be counted in cross-stitch on Ribband''™— strips of even-weave Aida fabric that come with scalloped edges finished in a variety of widths and colors. Surround the design with strips of different colored ribbons and lace and you have a professional look with no effort at all.

MATERIALS

Cotton floss
1½ yards watered silk ribbon ⅞″ wide
3 yards pregathered eyelet 1″ wide
16″ square white cotton
12″ artist's stretcher strips
1½ yard Ribband™ (*see* Suppliers)

ORDER OF WORKING

• Stretch white fabric over a frame (*see* page 129) and staple it in place.
• Trace the full-size pattern on to the center of the white fabric with Trace Erase™ pen.
• Separate the 6-strand floss and use 3 strands to work the dresses with long and short stitch and the sash bows and shoes with satin stitch.
• Use a single strand to outline figures with stem stitch. Work features with small straight stitches. Embellish dresses with single-strand buttonhole-stitch neck ruffles.
• Use 2 strands to work bullion knot "curls."
• With 6 strands, outline the basket with stem stitch. Use 2 strands to fill with long vertical stitches evenly spaced. Weave two full 6-strand lengths of floss over and under these stitches with a blunt needle.
• Fill the basket and crown the center figure with lazy daisy flowers and leaves worked with 2 strands of floss.
• Count the lettering onto the Ribband™ from

the graphs, working in cross-stitch with 2 strands. Baste in place around the design and miter the corners. Stitch a satin stitch heart (see pattern) over each mitered corlar. Choose the arrangement you prefer.
• Stitch 2 lengths of pregathered eyelet in place to create a double-ruffle "frame," as shown in the photo.
• Arrange the ribbon in a square shape, mitering the corners to fit over ruffles. Make bullion knot roses with lazy daisy leaves at each mitered corner. Tack ribbon over the ruffle to complete the design. Mount the finished place on stretcher strips as a picture or mount it as a pillow (page 137). The wording can be arranged as you like around the design, depending on whether you make the pattern square of rectangular. Choose whichever arrangement you prefer.

ENLARGING AND REDUCING

Most patterns in this book have been given in actual size. If a design does need enlarging or reducing, the best method is to have a photostat made. Photostat services are available in most towns (check your yellow pages under photocopying or blueprint services). Give one finished measurement, height or width, and the drawing will be enlarged proportionately.

Another method that can easily be done at home, at no expense, is enlarging by the squaring method. Generally, the simpler the design, the fewer the squares that will be needed. First, divide your design into squares as shown. Then take a piece of paper the size the englargement is to be and fold it into the same number of squares. (This is easier than measuring.) Draw the design square by square to fit within them.

USING A FRAME

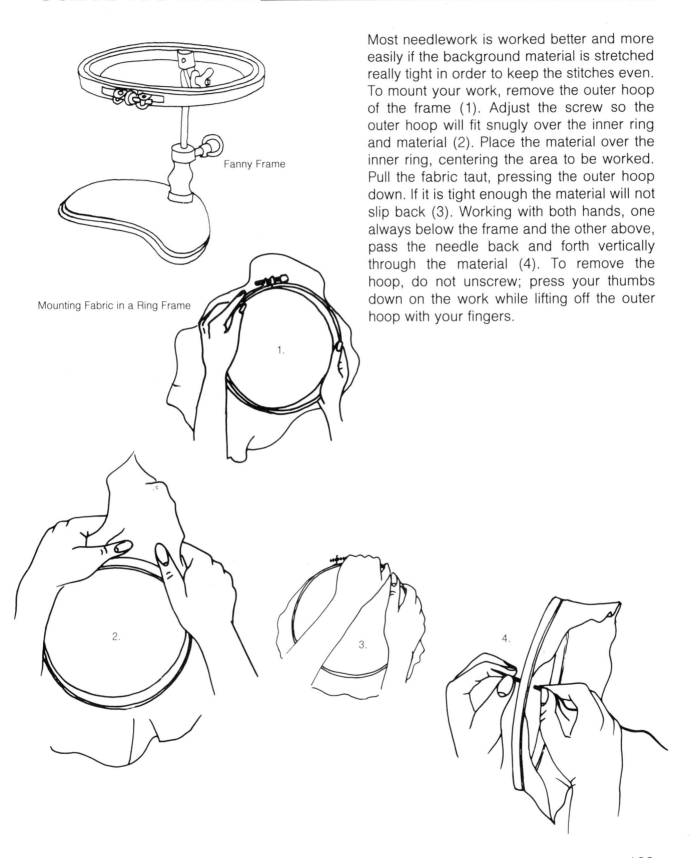

Fanny Frame

Mounting Fabric in a Ring Frame

1.

2.

3.

4.

Most needlework is worked better and more easily if the background material is stretched really tight in order to keep the stitches even. To mount your work, remove the outer hoop of the frame (1). Adjust the screw so the outer hoop will fit snugly over the inner ring and material (2). Place the material over the inner ring, centering the area to be worked. Pull the fabric taut, pressing the outer hoop down. If it is tight enough the material will not slip back (3). Working with both hands, one always below the frame and the other above, pass the needle back and forth vertically through the material (4). To remove the hoop, do not unscrew; press your thumbs down on the work while lifting off the outer hoop with your fingers.

BLOCKING

The best method for blocking finished needlework is by stretching it over artist's stretcher strips. This allows both sides of the work to remain exposed for cleaning and quick drying. Purchase strips large enough to fit around the outside of the needlework. Mark center of each strip with a pencil and assemble them so that each corner is a right angle. Mark the center of each side of the needlework and place the needlework on top of the stretcher frame, right side up. Matching centers, staple the four sides, stretching work tightly as you do so. Then staple the corners. Continue stretching and stapling around opposite sides until staples are ¼" apart and work is stretched square and tight. Run cold water over needlework and wash gently if it is soiled. Prop the frame up and let the needlework dry.

INSTANT FRAME

"Frame" large pieces of needlework (such as "Love Is a Shared Umbrella" on page 22) easily and inexpensively with grosgrain ribbon. Simply leave the piece mounted on the stretcher strip frame it was worked on. Tack grosgrain ribbon around the edges with a staple gun (or use white, clear-drying glue), making sure to turn under the raw edge at the end before tacking it in place. (To make a padded frame, see page 105.)

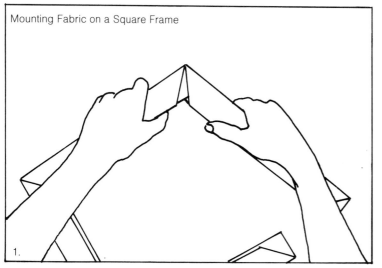

Mounting Fabric on a Square Frame

1.

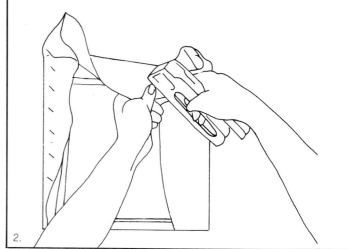

2.

TRANSFERRING

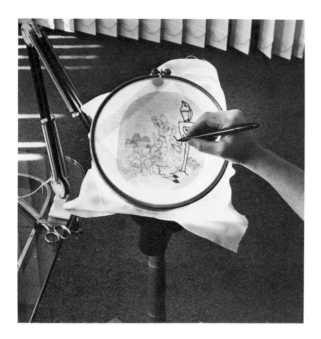

Back Lighting
(For medium-weight linen or cotton, velvet, delicate fabrics and blends)

Stretch fabric onto artist's stretcher strips and staple or track it. Tape a boldly traced design to the reverse side, close to the fabric. Place a lamp behind the frame so a clear silhouette of the design shines through. Trace with a fine-tipped permanent marker. (You can also tape the design and then the fabric to an artist's lightbox and then trace it.)

Carbon Paper
(For medium-weight linen or cotton)

Use only dressmaker's carbon—blue for light materials, white or yellow for dark. Working on a smooth, hard surface, slide a sheet of carbon face down between the pattern and fabric. Anchor with weights and, with smooth flowing lines, trace the outline heavily with a pencil.

Trace Erase™ Pen
(For all fabrics)

This marking pen transfers with a blue line that can be erased by touching it with cold water. It is ideal for freehand drawing because unwanted lines will completely disappear after the needlework is complete. Never apply heat beofre removing the blue lines or they will become permanent.

Tracing
(For needlepoint canvas, evenweave fabrics, and organdy)

Tape transparent fabrics directly over the design on a smooth surface. Lightly trace the design with a hard pencil. Similarly, tape needlepoint canvas over a boldly drawn design. Use a fine permanent marker to trace the design onto canvas.

Graphs
(For canvas and evenweave fabrics)

Some designs are counted directly from a graph on to canvas or evenweave fabric. Always work from the center out, counting the *threads* of the fabric—not the holes. One graph square represents one stitch.

Waste Canvas
(For most fabrics except canvas, evenweave fabrics, and organdy)

Baste waste canvas over the design area of the fabric and mount both in an embroidery frame. Stitch through both thicknesses as described above under GRAPHS. When the design is finished, unravel the canvas threas at the edges and draw them out one by one. If your fabric is washable, soak it in cold water to loosen the threads, allowing them to slip out more easily.

HOW TO USE TRACE ERASE™ FABRIC _____

Trace Erase™ is the newer, more versatile way to do needlework. It enables you to apply your design to prefinished items, such as tee shirts, sweat shirts, and towels and to work on stretchy or deep pile fabrics with ease. Just follow these simple steps.

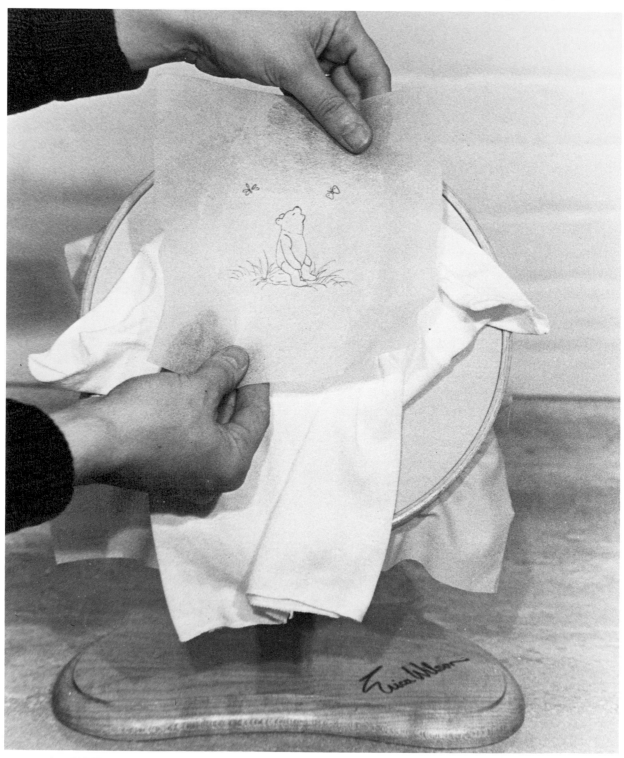

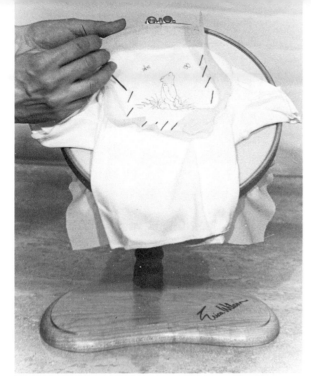

- Trace your design directly onto the Trace Erase™ fabric.
- Mount the fabric to be embroidered in a frame. For stretchy fabrics, such as the cotton-knit undershirt shown here, first mount muslin in the embroidery hoop, then baste the undershirt on top.
- Position the Trace Erase™ fabric with design on top and baste that in place.

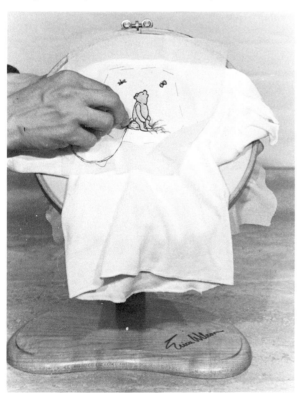

- Stitch design as you would any needlework, working through both Trace Erase™ fabric and lining.

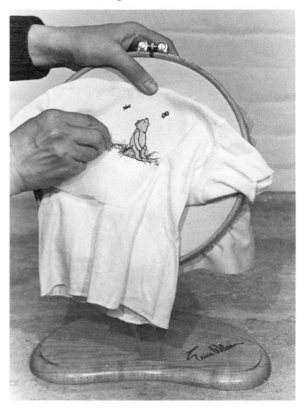

- Tear away Trace Erase™, removing any remaining bits and pieces by rubbing with the flat points of scissors.
- Your completed design will be perfectly neat, and no one will know your secret!

"COLORING BOOK CROSS STITCH" WITH TRACE ERASE™

The integrity of a drawing can be maintained by using this unique new method of working cross stitch. Instead of working out the design on the square grid, which results in angular shapes, outline the design following the drawing exactly, and then fill in between the outlines with cross stitches. Just follow these easy steps.

• Trace the design on Trace Erase™ fabric

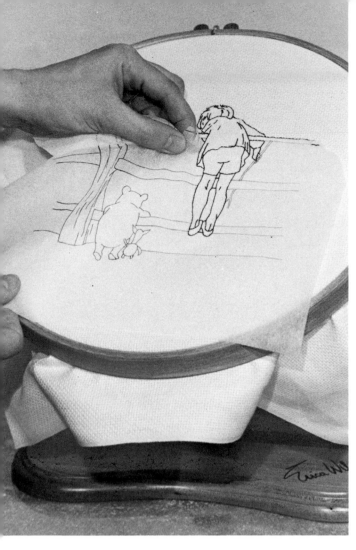

with a fine-point permanent marker.
- Baste in position on Aida cloth.
- Separate floss and work all outlines with 1 strand in backstitch, stitching right through Trace Erase™ fabric and Aida cloth. (Black was used here, to resemble pen and ink lines).
- Tear away Trace Erase™ fabric, revealing your "coloring book" outline!
- Simply fill in each area with cross stitch, compensating with small half stitches to fill in small spaces at the corners and edges. If you wish, experiment with novelty stitches, such as turkey work or horizontal long stitches, to highlight your "drawing."

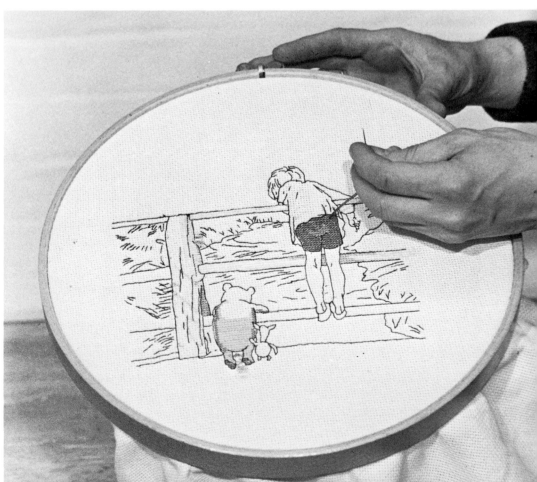

FABRIC MATS

Cut a piece of heavy cardboard to the desired size of the mat. Trace your oval in the center of the cardboard and cut it out. Cut fabric 4″ larger in both length and width than your cardboard mat, and stretch it tautly over the cardboard, taping the edges to the back with masking tape and making sure to miter the corners neatly. Slash the fabric almost to the edge of the oval as shown and tape fabric to the back. Place over your needlework and frame as desired.

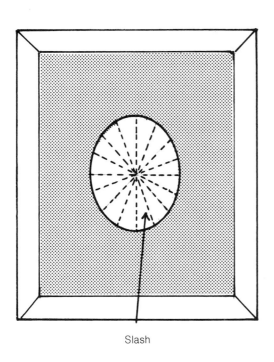

Slash

Tape

MOUNTING PILLOWS

FABRIC AND EYELET DOUBLE RUFFLE PILLOW

- Cut fabric for pillow backing, making certain to allow ½" all around for seam allowances. Trim front of pillow, leaving ½" seam allowance as well.
- Cut ruffle of desired depth (suggest 2½–3") and one and a half times the pillow perimeter in length (piece fabric with narrow seams as necessary). Cut eyelet the same length.
- Narrowly hem one long edge of ruffle. Place raw edge of eyelet along remaining long edge of ruffle and sew together with 2 rows of gathering stitches.
- Draw up gathers and pin ruffle face down around pillow front, with raw edges outward. Connect short ends with a narrow seam. Baste, then machine stitch in place.
- Place pillow back face down on front, enclosing ruffle to inside. Stitch around edge through all thicknesses, leaving an opening along one side to turn.
- Turn to right side. Stuff and slipstitch opening closed.
- If desired, cover cable cord with continuous bias and enclose in seam between ruffle and pillow front. Alternately enclose one edge of narrow grosgrain ribbon in seam for a lovely effect.

CONTRASTING FABRIC AND PLEATED FRILL

- Establish center of each side of finished embroidery by folding in four and marking with pins.
- Using the pins to help center the pattern, baste a rectangle around design with contrasting thread.
- On right side, lay four strips of contrasting fabric, right sides facing, to the inside of the basting line, allowing ½" turnbacks.
- Sew upper and lower strips first and fold them back. Then baste and sew the two side ones in place, and before folding them

back, crease down a 45° turnback from the seam line to the corner (as in diagram).
- Join strips at corners by sewing this 45° seam, right sides facing. Trim seam and fold back border all around.

When bordering strips are completed, set aside and work on gathering ruffle.
- With wrong sides together, fold a 5" strip in half and press. Gather or pleat so that the fabric reduces to half its length. Baste.
- Sew backing together with the ruffle and crewel piece as shown in the diagram. Remember to leave an opening at the bottom of pillow for stuffing.
- Stuff, and slipstitch opening closed.

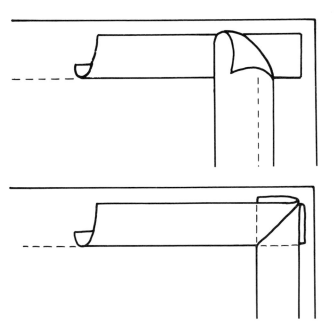

137

SELF-LINED TOTE

This tote bag has a useful pocket in the front that can be embroidered separately (*see* page 35). First, the pocket is secured by long ribbons, which also form the handles of the tote. Then the bag is made like a long sack, one end of which is pushed inside the other to form a self-lining.

MATERIALS

For Handles:	½ yard gingham (minimum width 27″)
	7 yards ⅜″ ribbon to match
	¼ yard heavyweight interfacing
For Pocket:	Fabric for embroidery (9 × 10¾″)
	Lining as above
For Bag Body:	Duck or canvas 16 × 59″
For Bag Sides:	2 pieces 6 × 25″ duck or canvas

ORDER OF WORKING

- Begin by making the fabric ribbon to surround pocket and form handles of bag.
- Cut and baste interfacing strip to measure 1½ × 108″. Cut 4 strips of gingham 27 × 4″. Join across width where necessary and lap over interfacing strip. Fold gingham around back and baste down edges on either side. Join into a ring and machine stitch ribbons in place on either side. Make identical short strip 9″ long for base of pocket.
- With right sides together, seam top of embroidered pocket and lining. Press, fold back, and baste the other three sides together, leaving raw edges.
- To position pocket on bag, mark and baste a line across the width of long body piece, 14½″ down from the top raw edge. Center and baste the finished pocket with its upper edge on basting line. Baste and machine stitch short gingham ribbon across bottom of pocket, overlapping ½″.
- Next, machine stitch ribbon to body of bag, surrounding the pocket as in diagram and overlapping it by ½″. Leave a free loop of 21″ for handle above the pocket, and an identical loop at the opposite end, to form the other handle.
- With right sides facing, seam short ends of bag together to form a tube (across 16″ width).
- To baste side pieces to body of bag, fold 6″ width of side piece in half. Mark center point with pin and line up with seam on bag body. Baste and machine stitch side piece to bag body all around. Repeat for second side, leaving 6″ open on one side for turning. IMPORTANT: When sewing sides to body, make sure not to catch handle straps, which are lying inside, in the seams.
- Turn inside out, slip in 5 × 15″ cardboard for base of bag, and slipstitch opening closed.
- Finally, push one half of the bag inside the other to form the self-lining.

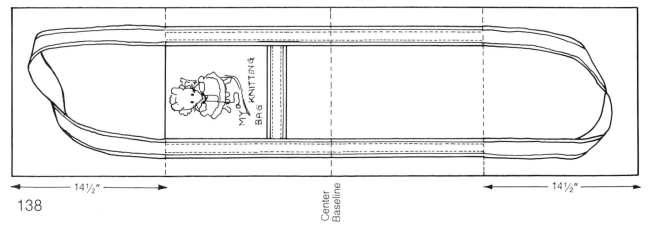

14½″   Center Baseline   14½″

STITCHES

RUNNING STITCH

Come up at A, go down at B and up at C, making a straight line of even stitches. The length of the stitches should equal the space between them. Several stitches can be taken up on the needle at one time, if the work is being done in the hand and not on a frame.

BACKSTITCH

Come up at A, go down at B, then up ahead at C. Repeat, going back into same hole as previous stitch. Keep all stitches the same size.

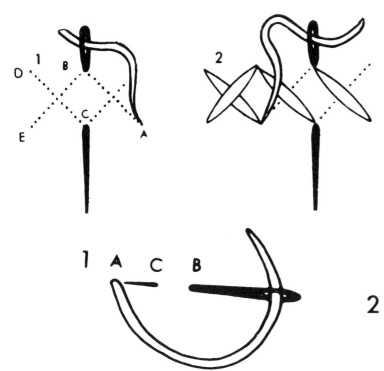

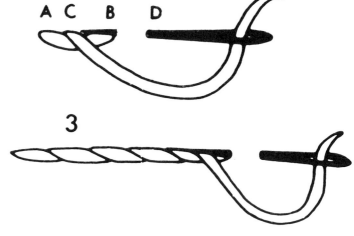

CROSS STITCH

1. Working from right to left, come up at A, go down at B, and up at C directly below B.
2. Return, working from left to right, going into same holes. Always keep the needle vertical.

STEM STITCH

1. Come up at A, go down at B and up at C. Keep thread below needle.
2. Go down at D and up at B (in same hole).
3. Repeat 2. Always keep thread below needle.

STITCHES

CHAIN STITCH

1. Come up at A.
2. Replace needle in same hole at A, forming a loop. Come up at B, inside the loop. Come up at B inside the loop and draw flat.
3. Repeat, always going down inside each previous loop.

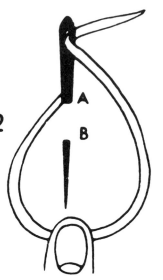

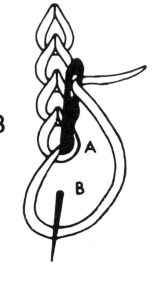

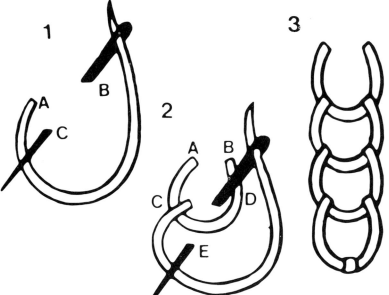

OPEN CHAIN STITCH

1. Make a chain stitch, coming up at A, going in at B, and coming up again at C, directly below A. Loop the thread under the needle as in the diagram, and pull gently through.
2. Repeat, going in at D *inside* the first chain stitch to the right and level with C, and up at E directly below C. Loop the thread under the needle and draw through gently. Note that the needle is always slanted instead of straight, as in regular chain stitch.
3. Finished effect shows a line of open loops.

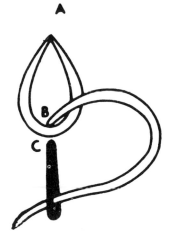

DETACHED CHAIN (LAZY DAISY)

Follow chain stitch steps 1 and 2.
3. Go down at C outside the loop to secure it.

140

SPLIT STITCH

1. Make a straight stitch, A to B. Draw flat.
2. Come up at C, splitting stitch A-B in Center.
3. Continue, making a smooth row of flat stitches.

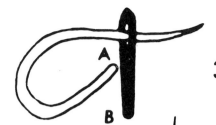

SATIN STITCH

For ease in keeping angle correct, start in center or widest part of stitch. Come up one side, go down on the other; cross over underneath and come up on first side again. Repeat, keeping stitches evenly side by side.

SATIN WITH SPLIT STITCH

First Split Stitch (D) around outline, then Satin Stitch over Split Stitches to form a smooth padded edge. Do not pull too tightly.

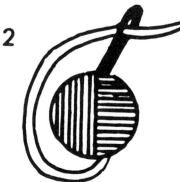

PADDED SATIN

1. Work Satin Stitch over whole shape.
2. Work second layer of Satin Stitches over first, in opposite direction.

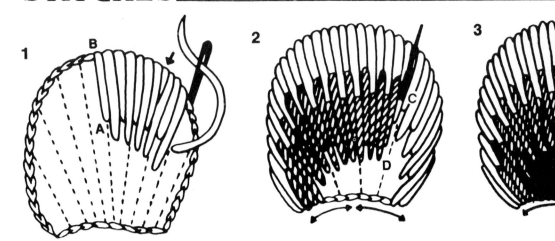

LONG AND SHORT STITCH/ SOFT SHADING

1. Draw guide lines in pencil on the material (as shown by dotted lines). Then outline the shape with Split Stitch, all around. Next work the first row of Long and Short, coming up at A and going down *over* the Split Stitch at B, starting in the center (or highest point) of each petal. It is easier to work downward from the center on either side, since the angle of the stitch is straight to begin with, then gradually fans very slightly on each side. To achieve this, the stitches may be placed slightly wider apart on the outside edge and closer in the center, exactly like a fan. If this is not sufficient, a greater slant may be obtained by taking an extra short stitch over the upper edge occasionally (as indicated by the arrow in the diagram). This "wedge stitch" will not show, providing the next stitch is taken extremely close to it. On the shape illustrated, few wedge stitches are necessary, since all the stitches gravitate to the center of the flower like the spokes of a wheel.

2. Work a second row of stitches in the next shade lighter or darker, coming up at C and down at D. Here again the stitches fan slightly, as in the first row. They should not change direction abruptly, but should flow into one another smoothly. As in Tapestry Shading, be sure to split far enough back into the previous row, and make the stitches long

enough for the third row to split into them. In the shape illustrated, this second row of stitches comes right over the outline at the lowest point of the petals.

3. With the third color, fill the remaining space in the center of the petal. Come up at E and go down at F. Bring the stitches evenly down *over* the Split Stitch, making a smooth outline, as at the beginning. On the third row it is impossible to fit each stitch *exactly* back through the previous stitch; every now and again miss one (as in diagram). This is because there is less space in the center of the curve than on the outside. Still, make the stitches look regular, keeping a long and short effect.

STRAIGHT STITCH

1. Come up at A and go down at B, making one straight stitch (like an individual Satin Stitch).
2. Stitches may fit close together.

FRENCH KNOTS

1. Come up at A. Twist thread lightly once around needle.
2. Return needle to same hole, draw thread tight, and push needle through.
3. Finished effect. To vary the size of knot, use 2 or more threads.

FRENCH KNOTS ON LONG STITCH

1. Come up at A, twist thread once around needle.
2. Draw tight and go in at B, about ¼" away.
3. Finished effect.

SEEDING

1 and 2. Take two little stitches on top of one another and scatter them in any direction.
3 and 4. Finished effect.

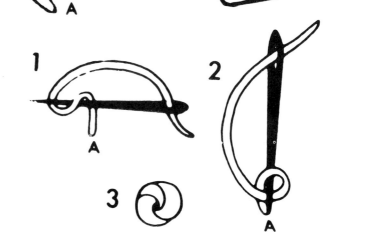

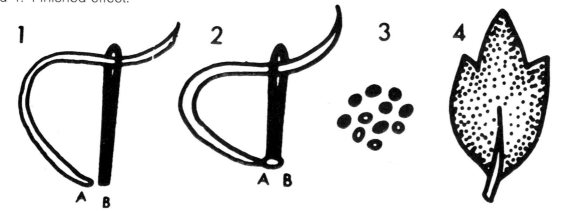

STITCHES

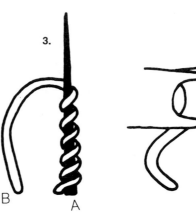

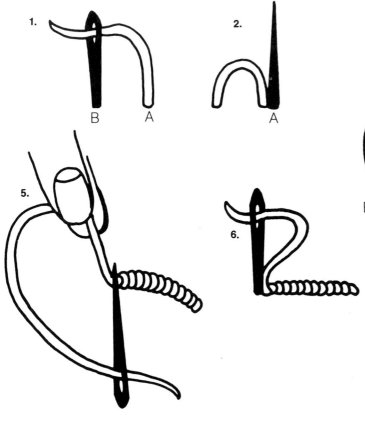

BULLION KNOTS

1. Bring needle up at A, go down at B, but do not pull thread through.
2. Stab needle up at A again but bring it only *halfway* through material.
3. Holding needle from below, twist thread around needle at A, until number of twists equals the distance between A and B.
4. Holding top of needle and threads firmly with finger and thumb of left hand, draw needle through with right hand, loosening coil of threads with left hand as you do so, to allow needle to pass through freely.
5. Place needle against end of twist, at the same time pulling on the thread as shown, until the knot lies flat on the material. If any "bumps" appear in the knot, flatten these by stroking the underneath of twist with the needle, at the same time pulling on the thread.
6. Put needle in close, at the end of the twist, and pull through firmly.

BULLION KNOT ROSES

To make a bullion knot rose, work 2 bullion knots side by side as shown. Then, work 1 bullion knot to wrap around one end, putting a few extra twists on it so that the knot curls around instead of lying straight. Next, add another bullion, overlapping half way over the previous one. Work in this way, until rose is formed as shown.

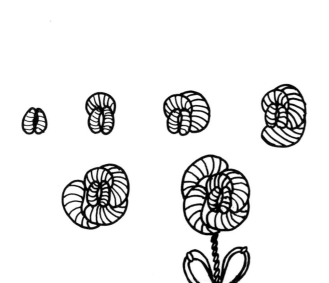

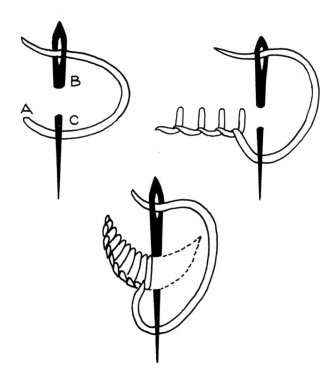

BUTTONHOLE STITCH

1. Needle comes up at A, goes in at B, and up at C directly below B and level with A. Thread is held under needle as in diagram. Draw through downward.
2. Next stitch repeats step 1 at an even distance apart. Stitching may be spaced as shown, or worked closely as in step 3.
3. Diagram shows angle of needle when working curved shapes.

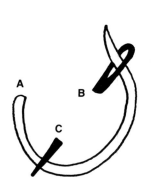

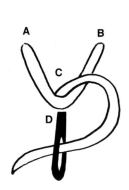

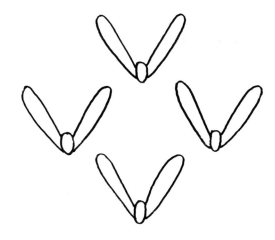

FLY STITCH

1. Come up at A, go down at B, and come up at C. Loop the thread under the needle as shown and draw gently through.
2. Go down at D, over the loop to secure it.
3. Finished effect.

STITCHES

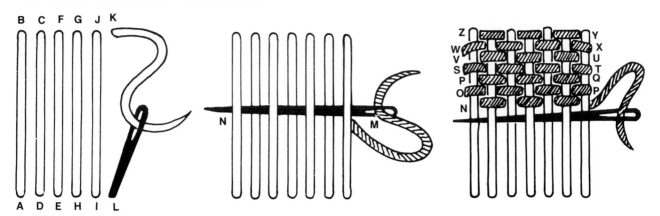

WEAVING STITCH

1. Come up at A, down at B, up at C, down at D, etc., laying threads side by side (the width of one thread apart).

2. Change to a blunt tapestry needle, and using a contrasting color, come up at M. Weave under and over the threads, darting through the center (or the widest part). Go down through the material at N.

3. Come up through the material at O, and weave through the threads, go down at P, up at Q, and continue to Z, pushing threads together so that even squares of each color are obtained. Go back to the center (A), and finish weaving the lower part.

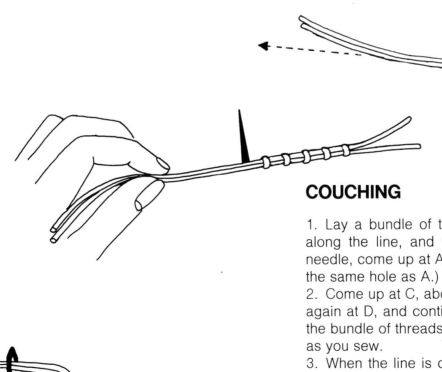

COUCHING

1. Lay a bundle of threads (in this case 3) along the line, and with one thread in the needle, come up at A, in at B. (B is almost in the same hole as A.)

2. Come up at C, about $\frac{1}{4}''$ from A–B, down again at D, and continue in this way holding the bundle of threads taut with your left hand as you sew.

3. When the line is completed, thread the 3 threads into a large-eyed needle, plunge them through the material exactly in the hole made by the last couching stitch and cut them off short (about $\frac{1}{4}''$) on reverse side.

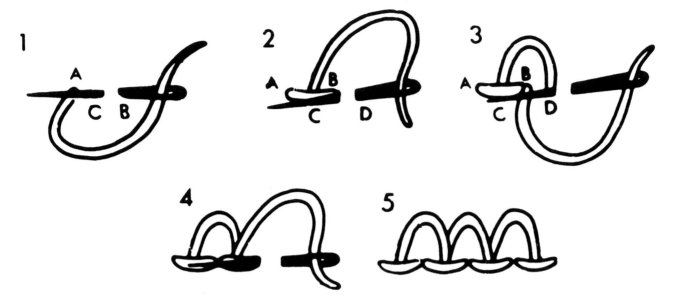

TURKEY WORK STITCH (UNCUT)

1. Come up at A, go down at B, and up at C halfway between A and B. Holding thread below needle, pull tight.
2. With thread above needle, go down at D and come up at B in same hole, leaving a loop.
3 and 4. Repeat, holding thread below needle and pulling tight, then above, leaving a loop. Keep loops even.
5. Finished effect of a single line.

TURKEY WORK (CUT)

1. Fill in area with straight rows of Turkey Work. Make small stitches and keep rows close together. Leave loops long enough to trim easily when area is completed.
2. Finished effect.

STITCHES

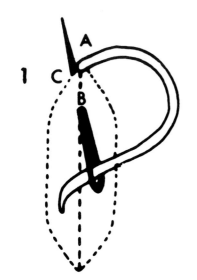

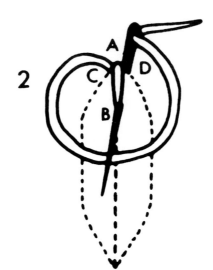

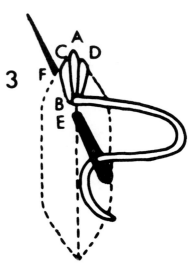

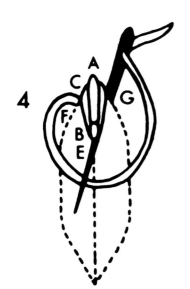

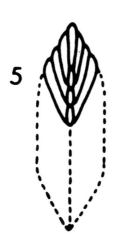

FISHBONE STITCH

1. Come up at A and go down at B about ¼″ below. Come up at C just below and to left of A.
2. Go down at D, just below and to right of A. Looping thread under needle, come up at B in same hole.
3. Make a generous stitch down center and come up on edge at left.
4. Repeat 2 and 3.
5. Several stitches completed.

FISHBONE OPEN

Work exactly as above Fishbone, but space stitches wider apart for effect shown.

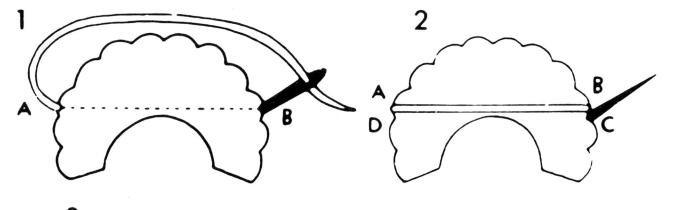

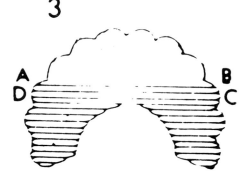

LAIDWORK STITCH AND
LAIDWORK TIED WITH CROSS BARS

1. Start in center or widest part of shape, and lay long stitches across it.

2. Come up the same side that you go down. (Practically no yarn shows on reverse side.)

3. Half of area filled in. Laidwork may be held flat in many ways by using other stitches on top of it in an opposite direction.

4 and 5. Hold stitches flat with crisscross stitches across shape. Make perfect diamonds.

6. Hold down with a stitch in contrasting color.

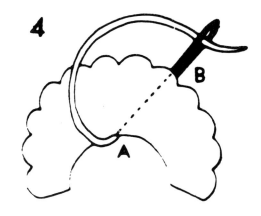

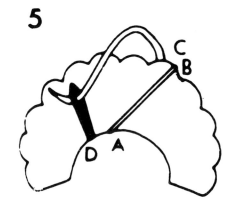

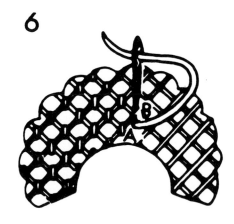

STITCHES

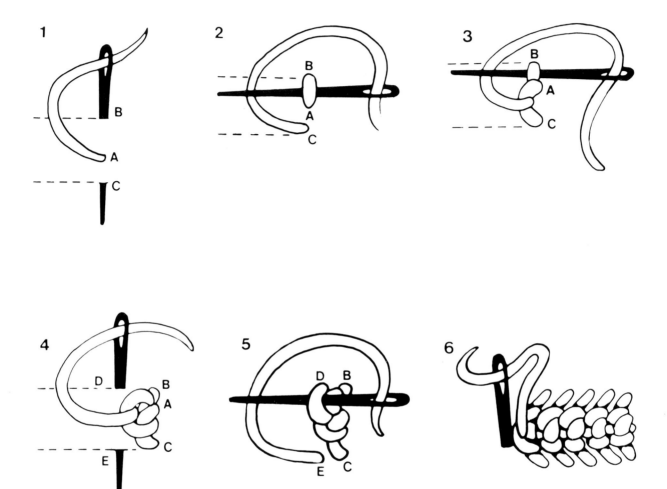

KNOTTED PEARL STITCH

1. Come up at A, go down at B, and up again at C. A–B–C are all on a straight line (as shown).

2. Using a blunt needle, slide under stitch B–A from right to left without going through material. Holding loop under the needle (as shown), pull flat. This forms one Buttonhole Stitch on bar B–A.

3. Now work a second Buttonhole Stitch by going under the bar B–A again, exactly as in step 2.

4. Go down through the material at D and come up at E. D and E are level with B and C (as shown).

5. Now repeat step 2 again. This time the Buttonhole Stitches are worked into the bar at D (as shown). Be very careful to pick up only the bar at D and not the other stitches.

6. Finished effect. To complete row, go down outside last Buttonhole loop to anchor it.

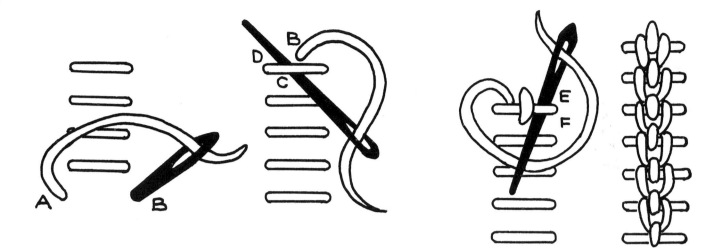

RAISED CHAIN STITCH

1. First work a series of parallel stitches (just under 1/4″ apart) as shown in diagram (as for Raised Stem Stitch).

2. Bring thread up at B and slide under thread from C to D. (Do not go through material.) This stitch is best worked with a blunt needle. Draw through and hold thread upward, keeping it rather taut.

3. Slide needle downward under same thread, but to the right of first stitch, from E to F, and draw through, holding thread under needle. Do not pull too tightly so the appearance of the stitch is as in step 4.

4. Continue stitch by repeating steps 2 and 3. Several rows may be worked side by side to fill a space (as in Raised Stem Stitch) instead of single row shown. In this case, end off row at base and start again at the top, ready to work downward.

HALF CROSS-STITCH

Come up at A, count one thread up and one thread over to the right, and go in at B. Come up at C, one thread immediately below B. The needle is therefore always vertical, as shown. Work to the end of the line, then turn the canvas completely upside down, and make another identical row below, fitting the new stitches into the holes made by the previous ones. Continue, turning the canvas at the end of each row. Half cross-stitch should always be worked on plastic canvas or double thread (penelope) canvas. The upright stitches formed on the reverse side cannot slip between the mesh, as they might on single or mono canvas.

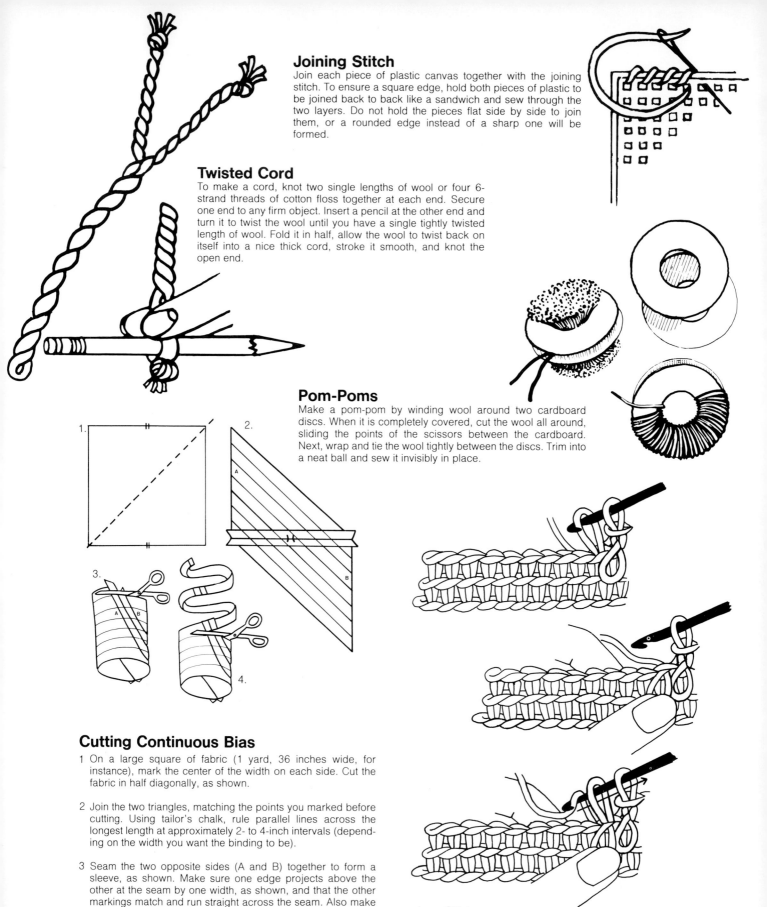

Joining Stitch

Join each piece of plastic canvas together with the joining stitch. To ensure a square edge, hold both pieces of plastic to be joined back to back like a sandwich and sew through the two layers. Do not hold the pieces flat side by side to join them, or a rounded edge instead of a sharp one will be formed.

Twisted Cord

To make a cord, knot two single lengths of wool or four 6-strand threads of cotton floss together at each end. Secure one end to any firm object. Insert a pencil at the other end and turn it to twist the wool until you have a single tightly twisted length of wool. Fold it in half, allow the wool to twist back on itself into a nice thick cord, stroke it smooth, and knot the open end.

Pom-Poms

Make a pom-pom by winding wool around two cardboard discs. When it is completely covered, cut the wool all around, sliding the points of the scissors between the cardboard. Next, wrap and tie the wool tightly between the discs. Trim into a neat ball and sew it invisibly in place.

Cutting Continuous Bias

1 On a large square of fabric (1 yard, 36 inches wide, for instance), mark the center of the width on each side. Cut the fabric in half diagonally, as shown.

2 Join the two triangles, matching the points you marked before cutting. Using tailor's chalk, rule parallel lines across the longest length at approximately 2- to 4-inch intervals (depending on the width you want the binding to be).

3 Seam the two opposite sides (A and B) together to form a sleeve, as shown. Make sure one edge projects above the other at the seam by one width, as shown, and that the other markings match and run straight across the seam. Also make sure that the raw edges of both the first seam and the sleeve seam are on the same side.

4 Proceed to cut around along the chalked lines to form one continuous bias strip (rather like peeling an apple).

Loop Stitch

1. Insert hook into st. Draw up loop.
2. Remove hook from loop and hold loop in place with thumb.
3. Insert hook into same st as before and work one single crochet.

MUPPET™ PANEL PATTERNS _____

155

157

SUPPLIERS

*Illinois Bronze Paint Company 300 East Main Street Lake Zurich, IL 60047	Stenciling supplies, acrylic paint, Accent Country colors
*Stencil-Ease P.O. Box 311 Jaffrey, NH 03452	Fabtex acrylic paints
Sam Flax 55 East 55th Street New York, NY 10022	Versatex acrylic paints, acetate
Erica Wilson Needleworks 717 Madison Avenue New York, NY 10021	Knitting wools and needlework supplies, Fanny Frames, Trace Erase™ pen, Trace Erase™ fabric
*Stacey Fabrics Corporation 38 Passaic Street Woodridge, NJ 07075	Trace Erase™ fabric
Joan Toggit, Ltd. 246 Fifth Avenue New York, NY 10001	Canvas, Aida cloth, waste canvas
*Sabra Supply Company P.O. Box 35575 Houston, Texas 77035	Aida cloth
*Columbia-Minerva Corporation Consumer Service P.O. Box 500 Robesonia, PA 19551	Fashion Ease plastic canvas
*Stearns & Foster Company Consumer Products Division Wyoming Avenue and Williams Street Cincinnati, OH 45215	Batting and fiberfill
*Fairfield Processing Corporation 88 Rose Hill Avenue P.O. Drawer 1157 Danbury, CT 06810	Batting and fiberfill
*C.M. Offray & Son, Inc. 261 Madison Avenue New York, NY 10016	Ribbons
M & J Trimming Company 1008 Sixth Avenue New York, NY 10018	Beads, rhinestones, trimmings
*YLI Corporation (formerly Yarn Loft International) 742 Genevieve, Suite L Solaria Beach, CA 92075	Rotary cutters, utility blades, cutting mats
*DMC 107 Trumbull Street Elizabeth, NJ 07206	Cotton floss
Patchmakers, Inc. 136 West 21st Street New York, NY 10011	"Almost Ready to Wear" Kits

*Designates a wholesaler who will supply retail sources in your area.

BIBLIOGRAPHY

Barker, Cicely M. *Flower Fairies of the Summer.* London and Glasgow: Blackie.

Brunhoff, Jean de. *Babar and His Children.* New York: Random House, 1966.

Brunhoff, Jean de. *Babar's French Lessons.* New York: Random House, 1963.

Grahame, Kenneth. *The Wind in the Willows.* New York: Charles Scribner's Sons, 1960.

Grover, Eulalie Osgood. *The Sunbonnet Babies' Book.* New York: Merrimack Publishing.

Lane, Margaret. *The Magic Years of Beatrix Potter.* London and New York: Frederick Warne, 1978.

Lane, Margaret. *The Tale of Beatrix Potter.* London and New York: Frederick Warne, 1978.

Milne, A. A. *Winnie-the-Pooh.* London: Methuen, 1926.

Milne, A. A. *Winnie-the-Pooh.* New York: E. P. Dutton, 1961.

Mitchell, Gene. *The Subject Was Children: The Art of Jessie Willcox Smith.* New York: E. P. Dutton, 1979.

Schnessel, S. Michael. *Jessie Willcox Smith.* New York: Thomas Y. Crowell.

Spielmann, M. H., and Layard, G. S. *Kate Greenaway* London: Adam and Charles Black, 1905.

ACKNOWLEDGMENTS

I wish to thank the following publishers who so generously gave me permission to include my needlework adaptations of their storybook illustrations in this book: Frederick Warne & Co., Inc., Random House, Charles Scribner's Sons, and E. P. Dutton & Co.

I would also like to thank Jim Henson Associates for permission to include the Muppets™ and Disney Productions for Winnie-the-Pooh.

I greatly appreciate the patience of my daughter, Vanessa, my son, Illya, and my grandson, Sandy Cushman, who posed as models.

Special thanks to Charles Scribner III for allowing his son to model in Color Plates 9 and 20.

Thanks, too, to JoAnn Moss for the crochet Babar toys in Color Plate 19.

The boy's suit in Color Plates 33 and 34 is used with kind permission of Bena Racine of the Patchmakers, 136 West 21 Street, New York, NY 10011.

Special thanks to all those who worked on preparing the book: Viola Andrycich, Mark Hamilton, Sonja Dagress, Elizabeth Kreid, Francisca Alvarez, and Luisa Cabrera.